Teaching Assistant's Handbook

S/NVQ Level 2

Heinemann
Child Care

Heinemann Educational Publishers,
Halley Court, Jordan Hill, Oxford OX2 8EJ
Part of Harcourt Education Limited

Heinemann is the registered trademark of Harcourt Education Limited

© Louise Burnham, 2003

First published 2003

08 07
10 9

British Library Cataloguing in Publication Data
is available from the British Library on request.

ISBN: 978 0 435452 12 4

Websites

Please note that the examples of websites suggested in this book were up to date at the time of writing. It is essential for tutors to preview each site before using it to ensure that the URL is still accurate and the content is appropriate. We suggest that tutors bookmark useful sites and consider enabling students to access them through the school or college intranet.

Typeset and illustrated by ⋏ Tek-Art, Croydon, Surrey

Cover design by Tony Richardson at Wooden Ark Ltd

Printed in China by CTPS

Cover photo: © John Walmsley

Acknowledgements

Every effort has been made to contact copyright holders of material reproduced in this book. Any omissions will be rectified in subsequent printings if notice is given to the publishers.

Tel: 01865 888058 www.heinemann.co.uk

Contents

Acknowledgements   iv

Introduction   v

Mandatory units   1
2-1   Help with classroom resources and records   3
2-2   Help with the care and support of pupils   29
2-3   Provide support for learning activities   53
2-4   Provide effective support for your colleagues   79

Optional units   **103**
2-5   Support literacy and numeracy activities in the classroom   105
3-1   Contribute to the management of pupil behaviour   143
3-10   Support the maintenance of pupil safety and security   177
3-11   Contribute to the health and well-being of pupils   193
3-17   Support the use of ICT in the classroom   211

Appendix   **225**

Glossary   **227**

Index   **230**

Acknowledgements

I would like to thank staff at Pickhurst Infant School at West Wickham in Kent for their support, particularly Gill Mallard for finding time to look at unit 4, and Ann Golding and Heather Mathews for reading through the Literacy and Numeracy section. I would also like to thank Zena Kellett for allowing me to reproduce part of the ICT Policy. Thanks also to Linda Holledge and Sue Mitchell for their help and advice with units 10 and 11.

I am also grateful to Alison Ballantyne from Bromley Behaviour Support Unit for her advice on Unit 3-1.

Thanks again must go to Mary James for all her help and to Penny Tassoni for her constant encouragement!

Finally thanks to Rosalyn Bass for guiding me through the final stages.

Dedication

This book is dedicated to Tom and Lucy, with love.

Photo acknowledgements

Gareth Bowden: page 6, 51, 138, 146
Corbis: page 10
Gerald Sunderland: 13, 118, 147
Haddon Davies: 41, 46, 57, 84, 89
Bubbles: 43, 69, 74, 159, 207
John Walmsley: 145, 215
SPL: 202

Introduction

Welcome to this Level 2 handbook for the National Vocational Qualification (NVQ) or Scottish Vocational Qualification (SVQ) for teaching assistants. If you are using this book you may be a new entrant to this occupation. This handbook has been written for assistants in primary schools, although if you are working in a secondary school you may find that many of the ideas and principles will apply to you as well.

You may find yourself referred to under the general title of 'teaching assistant' within your school, but you may also be called a 'classroom assistant', 'school assistant', 'individual support assistant', 'special needs assistant' or 'learning support assistant'. These different titles have come about due to the different types of work which assistants are required to do within the classroom. For the purpose of this book we will refer to all those who assist within the classroom as teaching assistants.

As an assistant, you will be required to carry out many different jobs within the classroom. At the time of writing, assistants are increasingly required to take on a more leading role alongside teachers and are being given more training and responsibilities. You may be one of a large team of assistants within a big urban primary school or you may be part of a much smaller team of adults in a village school.

Some background information about the NVQ

The structure of the NVQ level 2 requires you to achieve **seven** units of competence from the national occupational standards. You will need to complete each of the four **mandatory units** and three of the **optional units.** Since the optional units can be chosen, it may be useful for you to think about them in relation to your own job role and career aspirations.

In addition, you should know that:

▶ units 3–1, 3–10, 3–11 and 3–17 are also common with the level 3 award and credit for them can be carried forward if you go on to do this.

▶ each of the mandatory units and optional unit 2–5 contributes to the competence requirements for 2 of the level 3 units.

How to use this book

Each unit within this book has been written as a separate chapter. For each unit we have identified what you will need to know and understand and then given information and activities related to these items of learning. At the end of each element, there is an evidence collection activity which may help you when thinking about how to show competence for each element. There is also an end of unit test, which you can use to check your understanding. As each unit stands alone, this also means that you will be able to use them in any order, although when collecting evidence remember that it may sometimes be used for more than one unit since they do overlap. Where these overlaps occur, you will find cross-references within the book.

Throughout each chapter, there are a number of features to help you:

Knowledge into action

These are activities which ask you to check or try out ideas within your own workplace. They will help you to link your ideas with what happens in practice.

Find out about...

These activities help you to think more deeply about key issues and encourage you to carry out your own research.

Keys to good practice

These are checklists of the most important aspects of what you have just learned.

Think about it

These activities encourage you to apply theory in a practical way.

Case studies

These are examples within real settings where you can apply what you have learned to particular situations.

Evidence collection

These are to help you to collect evidence for each unit. They may be particularly helpful for those units in which you may need to use simulation.

Throughout the book, you will need to think about how the theory fits in with your experiences in the classroom. As you gain experience and expertise in your work with children, you may also find it a useful reference, particularly when thinking about specific issues such as literacy and ICT.

Values and principles underpinning the National Occupational Standards for teaching assistants

The national occupational standards for teaching assistants are built upon the following set of agreed values and principles of good practice:

▷ working in partnership with the teacher

▷ working within statutory and organisational frameworks

▷ supporting inclusion

▷ equality of opportunity

▷ anti discrimination

▷ celebrating diversity

▷ promoting independence

▷ confidentiality

▷ continuing professional development

You will need to consider these in relation to all the work you undertake within a school. For a fuller description of each of these, see the national occupational standards for teaching assistants, produced by the Local Government National Training Organisation. (LGNTO). You can find these on the LGNTO website: www.lg-employers.gov.uk. Under the A–Z listings, you will find a section called 'Teaching and classroom assistants' standards'.

Mandatory units

Unit 2-1 Help with pupil resources and records

There are two elements to this unit. These are:

2-1.1 Help with organisation of the learning environment
2-1.2 Help with classroom records

This unit is about how your can support the class teacher by helping to organise the learning environment. As a classroom assistant you will be working alongside the teacher, helping him or her by organising the classroom environment and supporting the introduction of new activities. You will learn about your role when organising different learning environments by preparing and setting out classroom resources and equipment. You will also need to consider health and safety issues within the learning environment and be aware of the kinds of situations which could present safety issues when working with children.

You will also need to have an understanding of the different kinds of records which you may be expected to keep when working in schools. These records may take a variety of forms and be kept in different parts of the school. You may be required to work with the class teacher to update records and need to be aware of issues such as confidentiality and legal requirements.

We all know that classrooms are busy places where children move around using various materials and equipment to complete their activities. Your supporting role in keeping the environment well-organised is very important. By keeping an eye on the materials, helping the children to manage the equipment and encouraging them to tidy up afterwards, you will play a significant part in creating a safe and productive learning environment.

Element 2-1.1 Help with organisation of the learning environment

For this element, you will need to know and understand the following:

▶ your role and the role of others when helping to organise the learning environment
▶ the principles and practices of inclusive education and the implications for setting out learning environments
▶ the school's requirements for health, hygiene, safety and security and how this affects resources and materials in the learning environment.

Your role and responsibilities within the learning environment

In your role as a teaching assistant, you will need to be able to supervise children in a variety of different learning environments and situations under the direction of the class teacher. This means that you will be working with children in other areas of the school as well as the classroom. (see Unit 2-3 for a more general outline of your role)

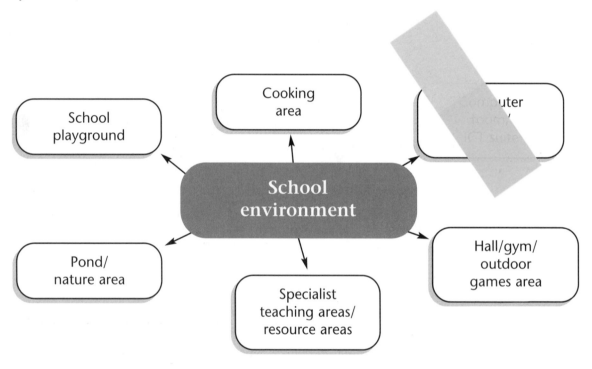

School playground

Cooking area

Computer

Pond/ nature area

School environment

Specialist teaching areas/ resource areas

Hall/gym/ outdoor games area

▲ The learning environment is more than just the classroom

You will need to be familiar with all these parts of the school before working in them, so that you are able to carry out activities with children. If you are asked to work with a group or class of children and are not familiar with a particular area of the school or do not know where it is, you should always ask for advice from others. It may not always be obvious that a particular area of the school is set aside for Science activities, or where you should go to look for Design Technology equipment.

The school should have resource areas where members of staff will have access to equipment for each particular subject area as shown in the table overleaf.

Examples of the kinds of resources that the school may have for different curriculum areas:	
Subject area	**Equipment and resources**
Science	Mirrors, a variety of materials, pipettes, magnifiers, water tanks, soil and flowerpots, torches, batteries
Maths	Clocks and timers for learning about time, scales for weighing, rulers and trundle wheels for measuring, coins for money, calculators, 2–D and 3–D shapes
Design Technology	Small saw, glue gun, split pins, dowelling, small wheels, cotton reels
Art	Different paints, pastels, different kinds of paper, wool and sewing materials, crayons, plasticene, coloured sticky paper, clay
Musical instruments	A variety of instruments such as shakers, drums and tambourines, instruments from other countries
PE	Large apparatus for gym activities, games equipment such as beanbags, hoops, a variety of balls, bats
Geography/History	Globes, maps, aerial photographs, artifacts for different topics, books
RE	Items from different faiths, books
Personal, Social and Health Education and Citizenship (PSHEC)	Books
ICT	CD-roms for computers, additional keyboards and mice, printers, recording and playback equipment, batteries

It may be very clear where some of these resources are, for example PE equipment. However, if there is a small subject area which you are not often required to help with or support, you may need to ask other members of staff. You should also make sure that you know how different items of equipment work before you come to use them.

 Knowledge into action

Find out where the following resource areas are in your school.

▶ Science

▶ Art

▶ Geography

Are resources for these subjects clearly marked and easy to find?

▲ You will need to know where to find different equipment in the school

Preparing learning materials

All primary schools will have a variety of materials which will need to be prepared for use on a daily basis. Some of these will be easily accessible, for example glue and scissors, but others may take longer to organise, for example where children are using different materials to make a collage. If there is more than one class in a year group, there may be several classes needing to use similar materials in the same week and class teachers will need to ensure that there are enough resources available.

Class teachers have responsibility for managing the room and making sure that there are sufficient general classroom resources for the children. This will include items such as maths, literacy or IT equipment, puzzles, resources for role play and other classroom activities.

If you are working in other areas in the school, it should be made clear to you exactly what resources you are required to use and where to find them. You should also be told where particular items are stored and whether you have access to storage areas and store cupboards. Teachers should also ensure that the items which are needed will be available at the time and that there will not be other classes using the resource area. Some schools may have rotas and procedures in place for ensuring that all classes have equal access to resources and facilities.

✔ Use the amount of materials required for the number of children – remember that children can share some items.

✔ Be safe when using tools and equipment – try and think ahead.

✔ Keep waste of materials to a minimum – for example use paper and keep off cuts for other activities.

✔ Return materials and equipment correctly after use and encourage children to do the same – make sure they are put away tidily and in the right place, especially potentially dangerous items such as scissors.

✔ Report shortages in materials to the appropriate person.

✔ Dispose of waste materials safely.

The roles and responsibilities of others in the learning environment

Although everyone within a school will have responsibilities for maintaining the learning environment, some will have specific responsibilities and you will need to know who they are.

Health and Safety Representative – this member of staff has responsibility for making sure that there are systems and routines in place to maintain the safety of everyone within the school. You should be aware of the Health and Safety representative and the procedures for reporting any concerns to him or her. Health and safety will be discussed in more detail on page 14 and in Chapter 3-10 on page 175.

School Keeper or Caretaker – this member of staff works alongside the safety representative to maintain a safe environment. He or she will also be responsible for making sure that the general environment is kept in a safe condition, for example that minor repairs are undertaken as and when they happen, or that items such as light bulbs are replaced where necessary. The school may have a maintenance book so that members of staff can report any issues as they arise. Caretakers may also help with preparing larger items for use within the learning environment, for example using a video or overhead projector.

Facilities Committee – this part of the school's governing body is responsible for the school site and grounds. The committee will meet to discuss issues such as the repair and maintenance of the school. They will oversee contracts for people such as cleaners and gardeners who come to the school and will also make sure that Health and Safety guidelines are being met. Governors from this committee may include the teacher

▲ The school caretaker helps to maintain the school environment in a number of ways

governor and will always include the headteacher (see also page 81 – the role of the governor).

Subject managers or co-ordinators – these members of staff are responsible for making sure that their subject area has all the resources required. For example, the Art Co-ordinator will need to keep up to date on the amount of paints or pencils which are being used at any given time. They may have their own systems in place for doing this and you will need to find out how to report shortages to them. The different subject co-ordinators will need to make sure that there are enough resources if particular activities have been planned for a whole year group, such as working with clay.

Person responsible for maintaining stocks of materials – this member of staff will need to be aware of the kinds of resources which are used on a daily basis and which may be quickly used up. These will be items such as paper for photocopying, sharpeners and rubbers, chalks or pens for whiteboards, exercise books, staples and so on. You should make sure that you know who this is so that you can report any shortages when you find them.

Knowledge into action

Find out what records are kept in your school for recording stocks of materials. Who is responsible for ordering stock?

Principles and practices of inclusive education and its implications for setting out learning environments

Principles of inclusive education

At the time of writing, there is much work going into the promotion of inclusion in mainstream schools. This means that more children with Special Needs and disabilities are to be educated alongside their peers wherever possible. The reasons for this are:

1 Human rights

▷ All children have a right to learn and play together.

▷ Children should not be discriminated against due to learning difficulties or disabilities.

▷ Inclusion is concerned with improving schools for staff as well as for pupils.

2 Equal opportunities in education

▷ Children do better in inclusive settings, both academically and socially.

▷ Children should not need to be separated to achieve adequate educational provision.

▷ Inclusive education is a more efficient use of educational resources.

3 Social opportunities

▷ Inclusion in education is one aspect of inclusion in society.

▷ Children need to be involved with all of their peers.

As a result of this, schools may be in the process of writing or reviewing their policies concerning equal opportunities and inclusion. There may also be more assistants in schools supporting children with statements of special educational needs. You should be familiar with your school's policies on inclusion and equal opportunities.

Inclusion also means that all staff should be aware of those children who have specific needs, wherever they are in the school. For the Special Needs Co-ordinator, this may mean speaking to staff as and when children with special needs come into the school and perhaps displaying photographs in the staff room so that all staff are aware of their needs.

SEN and Disability Act 2001

The main principle of inclusive education is that all children have the right to be educated alongside their peers in a mainstream school wherever possible. This will include children who have Special Educational Needs or a disability which means that they have been educated in another setting or away from 'mainstream' schools. The SEN and Disability Act 2001 makes significant changes to the educational opportunities which are available to disabled children and those with Special Educational Needs. This means that it will be more likely for these children to be accepted into mainstream schools. There will always be some children for whom mainstream education is not possible, for example where highly specialised provision is needed, but the basis of inclusion is that the majority of children should not need to be separated from one another in order to be educated.

Inclusion promotes the participation of all in society	
Separation	**Inclusion**
'Special' or different treatment	Equality – all children to receive the support they need to build on and achieve their potential.
Learning helplessness	Learning assertiveness
Participation of some	Participation of all
Builds barriers in society	Involves all members of society

The Disability Discrimination Act 1995

The Disability Discrimination Act 1995 covered a range of services but did not include education. From September 2002, this Act was amended to include education and cover the following:

▷ to make it unlawful for schools to discriminate against disabled pupils and prospective pupils in admissions

▷ a requirement for schools and LEAs (Local Education Authorities) to develop a plan to make schools improve access to the environment, curriculum and written information for disabled pupils

▷ a duty for schools to ensure that they do not put disabled pupils at a disadvantage.

Case study

Freya is a child with mild special educational needs who is in a mainstream school with a support assistant. She is very small for her age and immature in both her social and academic skills. Freya is quite shy and aware that she is 'different' from the other children.

1 In what ways is Freya benefiting from being at a mainstream school?

2 How might the other children benefit?

3 What considerations might need to be taken when setting out the learning environment?

The implications of inclusion when setting out learning environments

Environmental Factors

When preparing the learning environment it is important to remember that the focus of the activities is always the children. You may find that you have set up an activity to work on with a group and that materials are not accessible to all children. Assistants who support individual children with Special Educational Needs will be aware that it is vital to be able to focus on the needs of every child.

As far as possible, children should all be given equal opportunities and this should be remembered in the learning environment. All children, including th Educational Needs, should be considered when planning and resources. The environment may often need to be adapted for children within the class.

Factors which need to be considered include:

Light – where there is a visually impaired child, the light may need to be adjusted or teaching areas changed if his or her eyes are light sensitive.

Accessibility – a child in a wheelchair or restricted mobility needs to have as much access to classroom facilities as other children. Furniture and resources may need to be

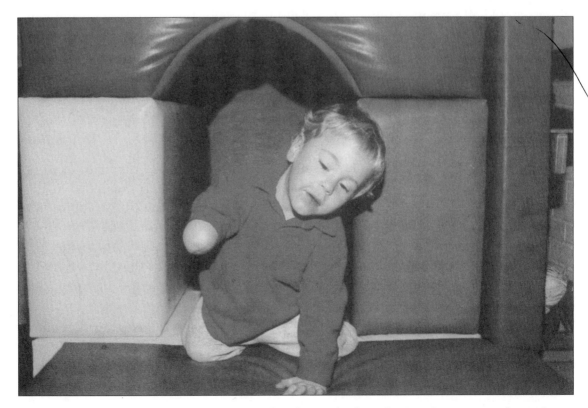

▲ Children with special needs may need to have the learning environment adapted

moved to allow for this. Children will also need to be able to reach and use toilets, turn on taps and access drinking water.

Sound – some children may be sensitive to sounds in the learning environment, for example an autistic child may be disturbed by loud or unusual noises. It is not always possible for these kinds of noises to be avoided, but assistants need to be aware of the affect that they can have on children and where possible to warn them, for example before a fire practice.

Movement around the school – children will need to be able to use all learning environments in the school which means that they will need to be able to move around without problems. Some older buildings may have difficulties with stairs, narrow doorways and toilet facilities but new buildings need to have provision for disabled people to include ramps, handrails and wheelchair access.

Health, hygiene, safety and security and their affect on resources and materials in the learning environment

It is important that you are aware of health and safety issues when working with children. As a teaching assistant, you have a duty to keep children safe, as they may not recognise potential hazards or be able to predict the consequences of their actions. All children should be able to explore their learning environment safely.

Your school will have procedures and policies in place for Health and Safety and you will need to be aware of these. (see also Unit 3-10 on page 177) There may also be guidelines for Health and Safety from the Local Education Authority (LEA). Schools need to encourage all staff to be vigilant and to make sure that accidents are avoided wherever possible.

First Aid

Assistants should know the location of safety equipment and First Aid boxes in school and the identity of trained First Aiders. First Aiders are strongly recommended in all educational establishments and need to have completed a training course approved by the Health and Safety Executive (HSE), which is valid for three years. The school's trained first aider should be responsible for ensuring adequate supply and regular restocking of the first aid box. Supplies should be date stamped as they are received as they have a five year shelf life. If you find that there is not sufficient equipment, this should be reported to the health and safety officer.

There is no mandatory requirement for the contents of First Aid boxes but they should include certain items as shown overleaf:

First aid boxes should include:

- a leaflet giving general advice on first aid
- 20 individually wrapped sterile adhesive dressings (assorted sizes)
- two sterile eye pads
- four individually wrapped triangular bandages
- six safety pins
- six medium-sized individually wrapped unmedicated wound dressings
- disposable gloves

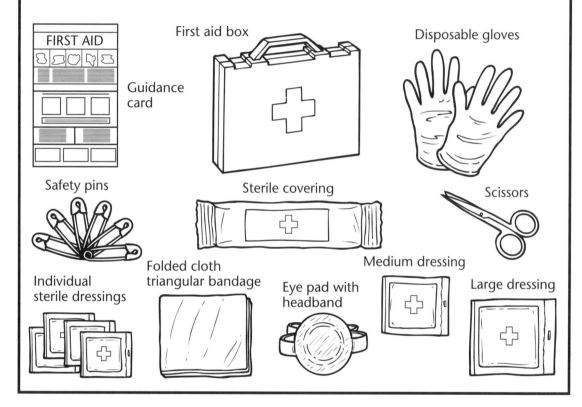

FIRST AID — Guidance card

First aid box

Disposable gloves

Safety pins

Sterile covering

Scissors

Individual sterile dressings

Folded cloth triangular bandage

Eye pad with headband

Medium dressing

Large dressing

 Knowledge into action

Find out the identity of the trained First Aider in your school and the location of First Aid boxes.

Safe use and care of learning equipment and materials

The school will have a Health and Safety policy which outlines responsibilities and requirements within the school regarding Health and Safety. This will also set out the

▲ How to hold scissors when moving around the classroom

school's guidance within the setting when dealing with health and safety issues. There should be information available on specific requirements in areas such as cooking, PE, First Aid, fire procedures and reporting accidents.

There may be separate sections for subject areas which have higher risk, such as PE and Science, and you should read these carefully.

You will need to be vigilant and look for situations in the learning environment which are potentially dangerous. These kinds of situations may not always be obvious. It is also a good idea to draw pupils' attention to safety issues which they can control within their environment, for example pushing chairs under desks when they get up or holding scissors pointing downwards when moving around the classroom. In this way they will start to develop their own responsibility for safety.

Sometimes, materials and equipment which are being used within the learning environment may have related health and safety issues, for example when using electrical equipment. This should always be handled and used according to manufacturers' instructions. You may require training and guidance when using some equipment and should also be given guidelines on the disposal of any waste following their use.

Security issues

You will need to make sure, particularly if you are working with very young children, that the learning environment is secure and that there is no chance of the children being able to wander off.

Remember – you need to be vigilant at all times.

Case study

Discuss in your group the following case study:

A child trips over a chair in the classroom and cuts himself on an open drawer.

1 What actions should be taken immediately?

2 What records should be filled in?

3 How could this have been avoided?

Keys to good practice
Safety in learning environments

✔ Train children to be vigilant.

✔ Keep classrooms and other environments tidy and organised.

✔ Always use safety equipment when required, for example goggles or gloves.

✔ Ensure children know how to use equipment which is rarely used, for example saws.

✔ Only give equipment to children which is age appropriate, for example glue guns should not be used by very young children.

Evidence collection

Alongside your mentor, look at and evaluate a learning area in your school and consider:

▶ Maximum use of space – is it being used efficiently?

▶ Accessibility for all pupils and staff – is everyone able to move around the learning environment?

▶ Good use of storage areas – are these being used so that all children and adults can reach learning materials?

▶ Health and safety issues – are there any obvious problems with safety? Look at fire exits, storage, electrical items.

Element 2-1.2 Help with classroom records

For this element you will need to know and understand the following:

▶ the range of record keeping systems used within a school
▶ roles and responsibilities within the school for maintaining record-keeping systems.

The range of record keeping systems used within a school

You may find that you are surprised by the number of different record keeping systems which schools are required to keep. It is very important that the correct procedures are used by all those who use and update records so that information is available as and when it is needed.

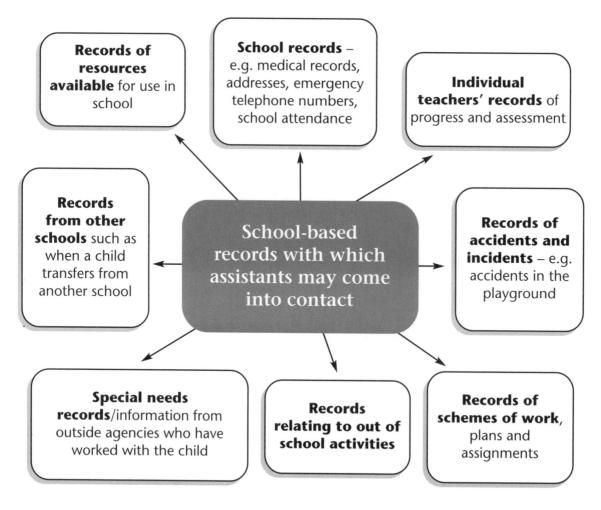

▲ Different types of school records

1 School records

Schools need to keep 'general' records on each pupil, for example medical records, records of attendance, names of carers and emergency telephone numbers. It is very important that these records are kept up to date, as they are usually collected when children enter the school and parents can forget to let the school know if they change.

Medical records will need to be updated and regularly checked, particularly when children have conditions such as asthma or diabetes. If medicines need to be given to children while in school, parents and carers will need to fill in a form stating the dose required and when it needs to be given. There should also be a record of how much medicine is kept in school.

Personal details will include names and addresses of parents and carers and usually details of another adult who can be contacted in case of emergency.

Attendance records such as school registers will need to be kept for 5 to 7 years. If children are absent on a regular basis without a written reason, these absences will be classified as unauthorised. These may be noted by the educational welfare officer who should visit the school regularly to check the attendance registers.

Pupil information form

Name .... **Date of birth** ....

Address ....

....

....

Tel. no. home ....

Tel no. work/mobile ....

Alternative tel. nos.
1 Name of person and relationship to child

....

Tel. no. ....

2 Name of person and relationship to child

....

Tel. no. ....

▲ Part of a personal details form

Records relating to out of school activities. Sometimes pupils will go off site to take part in activities such as swimming or they will go out on school trips. Records will need to be kept of parental permission given and telephone numbers of staff attending the activities in case they are needed.

Records kept by the school office for other purposes. The school will need to keep records of which children have participated or sent money when they are collecting, for example for school photographs or a sponsored event. Class teachers may have to collect the money and then send it to the school office and you may be involved with this.

Records of resources available for use in school. There should be records kept of the resources which the school needs to order on a regular basis or systems in place so that these are always in stock. These records will usually be kept by office staff but there may be different ways of doing it, for example on computers, on a card index or they may be automatically ordered at set intervals. Stock for individual subject areas such as art will be ordered by the subject manager.

2 Individual teachers' records of progress and assessment

These will be kept in the classroom and should contain the teacher's individual comments and assessments when working with children. These are important as they will help both you and the teacher when planning and carrying out work with children and will give a breakdown of each child's progress. They may also contain results of any formal national tests such as end of key stage SATS (Standardised Assessment Tasks) at the end of year 2 and year 6. They will also include copies of the child's school reports.

If you are asked to fill in class records for the teacher, it is important that you remember to complete them accurately and legibly. Look carefully at how and where others have recorded information and whether they have had to initial their additions. Always double check any records which you have to fill in.

Name: Nina Graham

Date:	Book read/page	Comments
6/9/02	The windy day	Read well. Good use of picture cues.
9/9/02	At the shops p. 2 – 7	Nina needs to follow the text with her finger so that she does not get 'lost'.
13/9/02	At the shops p. 7 – end	Good. Starting to read ahead.
16/9/02	Making cakes	Read through with no problems.
20/9/02	Where we live– p.8	Found hard to concentrate today.
22/9/02	Where we live– p.9 – end	Eager to talk about text, following with her finger.
26/9/02	Fun and games	Keen to read, but some difficulties with names in the text.

▲ Example of a child's reading record

Knowledge into action

Ask your class teacher if you can have practice at filling in a routine record such as the reading record on the previous page. How does the teacher usually do this? Are there other adults who come into the class who fill in records of readers progress?

3 Special needs records, information from other agencies

Children who have special needs will often be the subject of a lot of paperwork. This will usually be kept by the SENCo (Special Educational Needs Co-ordinator – see page 82 for an explanation of the other responsibilities of a SENCo) who will have their own system in place. The information which is contained in these records will usually be reports from professionals such as speech and language therapists, physiotherapists and class teachers. The records should be easy to find and filed or organised so that they can be referred to by all those who have contact with the child. It is unlikely that you will be involved with collecting this information, but if you are supporting a child who has special educational needs, you will need to see the records relating to the child. These may be:

Individual education plans/behaviour support plans – these give information about the kind of work which is being done with the child and targets which are worked on. (for an example of a child's IEP see page 34) All previous plans should be kept in the child's file. If you are working with a special needs child, you may be asked to help with setting up and reviewing targets along with the class teacher.

Reports from other agencies – these will give information from other professionals about specific areas of the child's development that give cause for concern, for example if the child has a hearing impairment.

Borough paperwork – this may vary between local education authorities, but your SENCo will need to keep paperwork on all children who have special educational needs which will document what the school has worked on.

School records – these will be basic information about each child.

4 Records of schemes of work, plans and assignments

These records will give a breakdown of the work that is being covered with the children during the term. There may be schemes of work broken down into subject areas and topic based activities to be carried out with the children. This will give a record of what each child in the class has been taught and the weekly or daily plan will include the learning objectives. You will not have to complete these but you may need to note down or fill in those children who do not achieve the learning objective or those who achieve it easily. This will save you writing something for each child and is called recording by exception. It might also be filled in on the short term or weekly plan, or simply on a class list to be transferred later.

Example of a topic plan for history – Year 6

Week 1 – Who were the Victorians? Introduction. Dates and Victorian timeline set up, to be filled in during the study. Talk about Victoria.

Week 2 – Education – visit by 'Victorian' teacher. Look at the work of Lord Shaftsbury and the welfare of children.

Week 3 – The Victorian home and the family. Look at artifacts and articles for use in the home. How the home is different now. Alexander Graham Bell and the telephone.

Week 4 – Health and hospitals – look at Florence Nightingale, the Crimean War.

Week 5 – Factories and industry. Isambard Kingdom Brunel. Transport and travel.

Week 6 – The Great Exhibition.

Week 7 – How the Victorians still influence us. Clues and reminders we still have today. Look at London street maps, place names, memorials, museums etc.

The learning objective for week 1 might be 'to place events and objects in chronological order'. Teachers will need to make sure that children have understood the timeline by giving them an activity to see whether they can do this. You may record whether the objective has been achieved by using a class list – see below.

Class list

Learning objective – to place events and objects in chronological order.

Achieved – all of red and blue groups, Gemma, Michael, Tim, Rebecca, Daniel. Anthony and Max found the activity difficult – need to work on chronological ordering.

Sara M could not complete the activity.

Caitlin and Sam were able to complete quickly and went on to do the extension activity.

Knowledge into action

Look at the way in which your class teacher records how children achieve the learning objectives during a chosen activity. Does he or she record by exception or keep notes for each child? Is this normal or does it change depending on the subject?

---

5 Records from other schools

When children transfer from other schools, the school will forward any records which they have about the child's achievement. This will be useful for the class teacher as it will give an indication of the level which the child has reached and the results of any tests which have been completed.

6 Records of accidents or incidents in school

There are times when you may be required to record details of an incident in school such as a child banging his or her head or one child acting aggressively towards another. The school will usually have an accident book, as there needs to be a record kept of any incidents, particularly if a child has been injured as a result (see also unit 3–10 page 191 for an example of an accident form).

Roles and responsibilities within the school for maintaining record-keeping systems

Different kinds of records which are held within the school will be the responsibility of different members of staff. Usually the majority of pupil records will be held with the class teacher, but others may need to have access to them.

Members of staff who will need to maintain pupil records

Headteachers	– to collect and collate school records including results of national tests and assessments.
SENCos	– to keep records of all children on the school's special educational needs register.
Subject managers	– to keep and monitor records of achievement in their subject.
Class teachers	– to keep records of their children's progress.
Office staff	– to update and check medical and attendance records within the school.

Headteachers, SENCo and subject managers will need to have a knowledge of pupil's records as it is part of their job responsibility to be able to report to others. This may include, in the case of the Headteacher, reporting to Governors and parents about the school's achievements. The subject manager will need to be able to report to the Headteacher and staff about teaching and learning in their subject. They may also need to monitor and moderate work, as well as looking at achievements and areas for development. The SENCo will need to keep detailed records so that they have access to concerns about a specific child.

Your role in helping to maintain records

You will not be responsible for maintaining records, but you may be asked to help teachers to keep them up to date and in order. Records which are medical or relating to special educational needs should be updated as and when changes occur since it is vital that the school has up to date information. If you support a child with a statement, you may be required to help with records for that child, although it is more likely that this will be done by the SENCo. Records which relate to the curriculum will be updated at least once a term or as planning takes place, and assistants should be aware of these but will not usually need to help with them.

Most records should be updated on a regular basis since they are working documents. For this reason, it is important to be aware of the school procedures for this. Records relating to assessment are the most likely to be completed by assistants and this may consist of a number of tasks including filing and transferring information. If a child has recently transferred from another school, information about them will need to be put onto the new school's records.

School policies for maintaining pupil records

The school should have an Assessment, Recording and Reporting Policy which will give information and guidelines about recording within the school. The system may be such that most of the school's records are kept on computer, so staff will need to be trained in how to use it. As an assistant, you may have opportunities for training with other staff and this will be important if you are to help them to update records. Even if you are not expected to do this, it will be useful to see how they are used and how information is kept within the school.

Knowledge into action

Find out from your mentor what kinds of records you may be asked to contribute to in school.

Confidentiality requirements

All staff who work in schools will need to be aware of issues concerning confidentiality. They will be building up the trust of parents, children and other staff with whom they work. You should remember that you should only access records under the direction of the teacher, or sometimes in the case of individual support assistants, the SENCo. The class teacher will need to be aware of the location of the records at all times due to the confidential material which they contain. For this reason, children's records should not be removed from the school.

You should not discuss children's records unless you are required to do so. It is important for assistants to ensure that any information which they are given is not passed on to other people. This is because the trust which has taken time to build up can be quickly damaged by a few careless words. There is also a legal requirement for schools to keep records of children and staff confidential.

 Case study

Katy is working as an assistant at an infant school for Hoi-Ming, who is autistic. Katy has just been working on some assessments for the class teacher and has read something interesting in a report from Hoi-Ming's mum about the kinds of things that happened when she was a baby.

1 Could Katy discuss what she has read with anyone else?

2 Are there any circumstances in which Katy should talk to anyone else about what she has read?

Keeping information secure

The school will need to keep information which it has on children safely. This will mean that you should make sure that any access you have to information and records is kept secure and only restricted to appropriate staff. They may have a policy for the storage and security of pupil records within the school and assistants should be familiar with this if they are dealing with pupil records.

Guidelines for keeping information secure

▷ Computer systems should not be left unattended when personal information is accessible.

▷ Passwords should keep information secure.

▷ Passwords should not be displayed in office or classroom areas.

▷ Discs and files should be locked away when not in use.

▷ Review and dispose of any unwanted personal data.

Legal requirements concerning personal information

You should be aware of the school's legal responsibilities when handling pupil records. Legally, personal pupil information should not be used for any other purpose.

According to the **Data Protection Act 1998**, information should:

▷ be obtained fairly

▷ only be kept for as long as is necessary

▷ be relevant to requirements

▷ not be used in any way which is not compatible to its purpose.

The Children Act 1989 requires that children's welfare must always be put first. It outlines some of the principles which need to be taken into account when children are being considered. Its main requirements are that children should always be consulted and informed about what will happen to them. Where a child's personal information is concerned, schools should ensure that this is only accessible to the adults who need this information.

The Statementing Process is the way in which schools send information to the local authority to decide whether a child qualifies for extra support in school. This information will be detailed and confidential and assistants who work with children with special needs will need to be aware of issues surrounding confidentiality (see page 24).

Keys to good practice
Maintaining pupil records

✔ Ensure you understand what you are asked to do.

✔ Make sure records are kept up to date and accurate.

✔ Ensure records are relevant.

✔ Maintain confidentiality at all times.

✔ Report any problems or breaches of confidence to the appropriate person.

Evidence collection

Think of a time recently when you have been asked to fill in a record. Note down the circumstances:

▶ Who saw the record and where is it now stored?

▶ Did you fill it in by hand or on computer?

▶ What, if any, were potential threats to confidentiality?

Keep a record of your notes and of the record you completed.

End of unit test

1 What does 'the learning environment' mean?

2 Name three different areas of the school you may be asked to work in with children.

3 What responsibilities does the school caretaker have?

4 What does 'inclusive education' mean for mainstream schools?

5 What policy will give you information about managing resources and materials safely within the learning environment?

6 Name four different kinds of record-keeping found in schools?

7 Who would be responsible for keeping records about children with special educational needs?

8 What should you do if you need to report an accident in school?

9 Name two requirements of the Data Protection Act.

10 How can you ensure that you keep all information confidential?

References and further reading

DFES, *Guidance on First Aid for Schools: A Good Practice Guide*

DFES, *SEN Code of Practice* (2001)

Paterson, G., *First Aid for Children Fast – Emergency Procedures for all parents and carers* (Dorling Kindersley/British Red Cross)

Index for Inclusion (CSIE, 2000)

Training for Inclusion and Disability Equality: *Disability Equality in Education* (2001)

Websites

Disability Equality in Education: www.diseed.org.uk

CSIE: http://inclusion.uwe.ac.uk
www.dfes.gov.uk/sen
www.network81.co.uk

Data Protection Act 1998: www.legislation.hmso.gov.uk/acts1998/19980029.htm

Children Act 1989: www.doh.gov.uk/scg/childrenactnow.htm

www.bbc.co.uk/health/first-aid-action/

Unit 2-2 Help with the care and support of pupils

There are two elements to this unit. These are:

2-2.1 Help with the care and support of individual pupils
2-2.2 Help with the care and support of groups of pupils

This unit will help you to demonstrate that you can provide individual pupils with the correct level of support which has been specified by the teacher. You will need to be able to show how you can do this whilst also encouraging the pupil towards building their own independence. You may be dealing with pupils who have special educational needs, behaviour plans or with those who need a little extra support to access the curriculum.

When dealing with groups of pupils, you will need to show that you can encourage pupils to interact with others in an appropriate and acceptable manner. You will learn how to take prompt action to deal with conflict or anti-social behaviour and when to refer these instances to someone else. You should also be aware of the limits of your responsibilities and be able to ask for assistance from appropriate staff when it is needed.

Element 2-2.1 Help with the care and support of individual pupils

For this element, you will need to know and understand the following:

▶ how to support individual pupils in the learning environment
▶ basic principles of effective communication and interaction with pupils and difficulties which may arise
▶ how to promote inclusion when working with children who have special educational needs
▶ your responsibilities for health, safety and security and child protection.

How to support individual pupils in the learning environment

When you are working alongside the class teacher, you will sometimes be asked to support individual children. This may because you are working with an individual child who has a statement of special educational needs. This means that the child's needs are such that they have extra support from an adult to be fully able to access the Foundation Stage or National Curriculum. It may also be that you are supporting a child in the class who needs extra help to enable them to achieve a particular task. You will need to be able to support the child in their work whilst encouraging them to be as independent as possible.

Whether or not the child you are supporting has special educational needs, you will need to use these strategies to ensure that you are supporting them effectively:

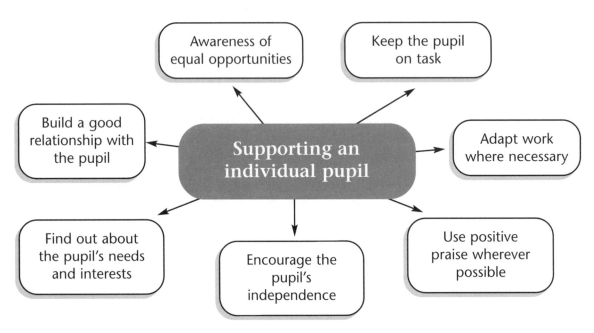

▲ You will need to use a range of strategies when supporting individual children

Build a good relationship with the pupil

Show you are interested in the pupil as an individual by listening to what they say and having time for them. You can do this by remembering to ask about personal things which have happened to them – how is their new kitten? – did their sister do well in her swimming gala? This is important because children need adults to take an interest and gain their approval. They may find some aspects of school challenging and it will be important for them to feel that they have someone who they feel has time to listen.

Find out about the pupil's needs and interests

You will need to find out what the child's specific needs are within the classroom in order to support them more effectively. These could be, for example a child who has dyspraxia and needs to work on exercises which help them to plan and carry out simple physical activities. You can find out about children's particular needs through the class teacher or SENco.

Case study

Brandon is a Year 3 child who has difficulties with organising himself. He finds it hard to remember instructions and doesn't always know what to do next. You have been asked to help Brandon by encouraging him to look at the last thing he has done and think what might come next.

1 Where might you find out more about Brandon?

2 How could you use this opportunity to build a good relationship with him?

Encourage the pupil's independence

Children need to be encouraged to be as independent as possible from the earliest stages of school. When you are supporting an individual pupil, this is what you are aiming for them to be able to do. It applies to their self-help skills such as putting on and doing up coats as well as to independence within their learning. It is important for adults to give children tasks that are appropriate to their age and stage of development. You will need to know how to provide support for a pupil whilst at the same time encouraging them to be independent.

Further strategies to encourage children to learn independently

As well as building good relationships and listening to pupils, you will need to:

▷ Give positive encouragement and praise – this will give pupils a feeling of achievement and desire to sustain their interest in learning activities. Children will be visibly boosted by praise when they are doing well.

▷ Listen carefully to pupils – children will be aware if an adult is only partially interested or paying attention to what they are saying. It is important to take notice of their contributions so that they feel they are being valued. In this way they will feel confident in their own abilities.

▷ Motivate pupils through positive experiences that are interesting and can be made real to them. Children will particularly enjoy and benefit from having artefacts and real objects to handle when learning. For example, children learning about a religion will remember more if they have seen examples of the kinds of items which may be used by a particular faith. These kinds of displays in classrooms are often the most popular and effective for children.

▷ Provide a level of assistance which allows children to achieve without helping them too much. This could be simply giving them a list of things which they may need to consider when carrying out a task or remembering not to give them help as soon as they ask for it. Try saying, 'have you thought about another way of doing this?' or 'are there any other things you need to remember?'

▷ Ensure that children have sufficient resources to complete the task so that they do not need to seek adult help. If you know that children are going to need particular items to carry out a task, ensure that they are accessible – or that children know where to find them within the classroom.

Use positive praise wherever possible

You will need to give as much praise as you can to build up the child's self-esteem and make them feel valued. When this happens, a child will be more likely to attempt to gain the same adult reaction by trying hard the next time. This applies not only to their work within the classroom but also to their behaviour. With very young children, you may also try positive strategies to draw attention to good behaviour, for example when they are all sitting on the carpet – 'Look how beautifully Sam is sitting', will immediately draw attention to the right kind of behaviour and often cause others in the class to do the same. In the same way, if you notice how hard a child has worked with an activity and you give him or her praise for doing it, the child will feel that it was worth making the extra effort.

Keep the pupil on task

The pupil may find it difficult to concentrate on their work for very long for a number of reasons. It may be that they are very young and unable to focus, or because they find the work challenging or it could be that they have ADHD (Attention Deficit Hyperactivity Disorder). This will make concentrating very difficult for them and you will need to give them as much encouragement as possible. You should do this by noticing when they are working hard and staying on the task. If the work really is too hard for the child and they are becoming frustrated, you will need to tell the class teacher.

Case study

Mark has difficulty with staying focused on his work and tends to try to distract others. Today the task is drawing a Greek vase and then decorating it. Mark has worked well for 5 minutes but then begins to lean over Ethan, sitting next to him, to see what he's doing. The teaching assistant intervenes:

Teaching Assistant: Mark, your vase is coming along very nicely. There's no need to look at Ethan's – what don't you colour it in now?

Mark: What's on your vase, Ethan?

Teaching Assistant: (persists) What's the design on your vase, Mark? Is it an animal?

Mark: (beginning to move back towards his own drawing) Well, it's supposed to be a flying horse.

Teaching Assistant: That's lovely – what colour would you like your horse to be?

1 How did the teaching assistant encourage Mark to stay on task?

2 Was this strategy successful or not?

3 Why do you think so?

4 What other strategies could the teaching assistant have used?

Knowledge into action

Find out if you can observe an assistant working with a child who has special educational needs. Which of the strategies on page 32 can you see being used?

Adapt work where necessary

The pupil may need to have work adapted if they are unable to cope with the work carried out with the rest of the class. Children who are working at different levels within the class will need to have their work differentiated. This means that they will all be working at a different pace from each other to ensure that the more able are challenged and the less able do not become frustrated. If you are working with a child whose needs are very different from others, you may need to make sure that their work is adapted. An example of this might be if you are working together on a simple number activity and you discover that the child finds the numbers too large.

Awareness of equal opportunities

You should be aware when working with individual children that all children should have the same opportunities in school, regardless of ability, race or gender. This is important and the school will have an equal opportunities policy outlining their commitment to equal opportunities for all and access to the school for disabled people.

Individual Education Plans/Behaviour Support Plans

These documents may be needed for children who have special needs, to help the staff and the pupil to focus on areas for development. They will usually be reviewed by all staff who are working with the pupil and also by parents, so that they are aware of the child's targets and the progress they are making.

Individual Education Plan

Name: Richard Jordan   School Action
Area/s of concern: behaviour, concentration   Start date: Jan 2003   Review date: March 2003
Class teacher: Mrs Fletcher   Year 2F   IEP no: 1
Support by: Teaching Assistant when possible   D/O/B: 11/11/96   Support began: Jan 2003

Targets to be achieved	Achievement Criteria	Possible resources	Possible class strategies	Ideas for assistant	Outcome/ review
1. To sit and listen when on the carpet.	Achieved on 2 occasions out of 3 by review date.		Sit Richard close to teacher. Sit away from distractions.	Praise good behaviour.	Not consistent, but much improved – still needs work.
2. To maintain attention in a small group activity and behave appropriately.	To participate fully in an activity for 10 minutes.	Playing games in a small group with assistant. Taking turns.	Talk to class about importance of taking turns. Give opportunities for Richard to share without constant reminders.	Encourage Richard to participate in games with others.	Now able to share without constant reminders – big improvement.

Parent/carer contribution: to work with Richard on related activities at home. Practice turn-taking with brother. Play games.

▲ An example of an Individual Education Plan

Case study

Jenny is in Year 1 and is very quiet. The class teacher has asked you to encourage her to communicate whenever possible as she tries to avoid speaking to others.

1 How can you do this without making Jenny feel that she is being picked on?

2 What strategies could you use?

Effective communication and interaction with pupils and difficulties which may arise

When building effective relationships with pupils, you must be able to communicate effectively with them. You should know the stages of language development which are expected of children so that you will know what to expect of children at different ages. If you are working with special needs pupils, this may mean that methods of communication are different from those used with other children. This may be because of speech and language difficulties, a communication disorder such as autism or because the child is hearing impaired and needs to use sign language. Some children may not speak at all and you will need input from others such as the class teacher or a speech and language therapist if you are working with a child in this situation.

Stages of language development in children	
Age	**Stage of development**
0–6 months	Babies will try to communicate through crying, starting to smile and babbling. They will start to establish eye-contact with adults.
6–18 months	Babies start to speak their first words. They will start to use gestures to indicate what they mean. At this stage, they will be able to recognise and respond to pictures of familiar objects.
18 months–3 years	Children will start to develop their vocabulary rapidly. They will start to make up their own sentences. At this stage, children will enjoy simple and repetitive rhymes and stories.
3–8 years	Children will start to use more and more vocabulary and the structure of their language may become more complex. As children develop their language skills, they will be able to use language in a variety of situations.

Communicating effectively with children

Whether you are working with a child who is just starting school or with an older child, you will need to think about the best ways of communicating effectively.

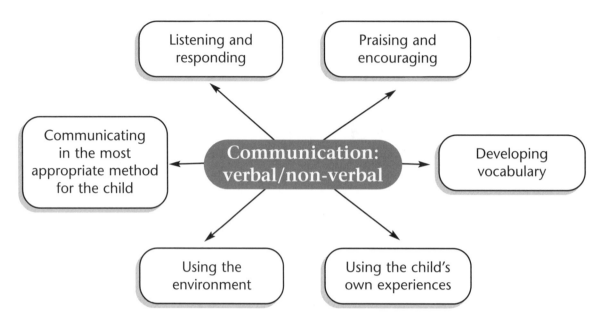

▲ Communicating with children effectively

Communication is a process which takes place on a number of different levels. When communicating with children, you will need to be aware of how important it is to think about them as individuals and respond appropriately. You should be aware that communication with others can be both **verbal** and **non-verbal**.

Verbal

This interactive part of the communication process involves listening and responding to what others are saying. In schools it is often referred to as 'Speaking and Listening'. For it to take place effectively, you will need to have time to hear, think and respond. Children will usually find it easier to speak than to listen and many of them will need to learn to listen to others.

The main principle of communication is that it is a two way process. For communication to be effective between you and the children, you will need to show that you are listening to them and valuing what they are saying. Sometimes this can be difficult in a busy classroom, particularly if you are working with younger children who all want to speak at once! You will need to acknowledge that the child is speaking to you and make sure that you respond to them, even if you cannot do this straight away.

Ways in which you can encourage children to communicate effectively with others may include:

▷ making sure you actively listen and respond to what they are saying

▷ use open ended questions so that children need to give full answers

▷ teaching them to reflectively listen, or repeat back what they have heard. This will encourage them to check their understanding.

You also need to be aware that young children can sometimes say things that may appear funny or inappropriate. You should be careful in the way you respond to this as you may inadvertently make children feel that what they are saying is not valued by adults, or is seen as amusing.

Keys to good practice
Speaking and listening

✔ Make sure you look interested in the person you are communicating with.

✔ Use open-ended questions where possible.

✔ Speak clearly and face the child.

✔ Respond appropriately.

Knowledge into action

Observe a speaking and listening session, either in your own or a different class. Look at how the class teacher encourages children to speak and listen to others. What kinds of strategies does he or she use with the children? Share these with your group.

Non-verbal communication (body language)

Body language can be seen as a very powerful communicator. Through it we can often tell how someone is feeling without speaking to them. We can also use it to communicate with others. There are several different ways in which we can give messages to others using body language.

Facial expressions and eye contact can be very useful when in a classroom. You may only need to look at a child to show approval or disapproval. When the teacher is talking to the class, or when children are working, you can often show a child that you are aware of what they are doing and encourage or discourage them to continue.

Think about it

Think about how often you use facial expressions to show approval and disapproval during the day.

Body stance can be used to communicate with others. Standing over children can be intimidating for them and even threatening if you have your hands on your hips. In a classroom situation, you may find that you need to crouch down to communicate effectively with children who are sitting at tables and chairs. Always sit or crouch if you can, as you can hurt your back by continually bending to talk to seated children.

Gestures can be used to show others what you are saying. By pointing, shrugging our shoulders or giving a thumbs up, we can add more weight to what we want to communicate.

Touch should be avoided in schools although this can at times be very difficult, particularly if you are working with very young children. Children will often approach adults for reassurance or help when they are upset and need to be comforted. Similarly, you may need to attract a child's attention or encourage them to listen. However, it can sometimes be misinterpreted. Your school should have some kind of policy on touch and you will need to be aware of it.

Sign language is a form of communication which may also be used in schools with children who have special educational needs. You may find that you have the opportunity to go on courses to teach you methods of signing such as Makaton or British Sign Language.

Knowledge into action

In small groups, take turns in demonstrating non-verbal communication using eye-contact, facial expression and body language. Individually and randomly role play the statements below.

1 Thank you.

2 That's enough!

3 What do you think you are doing?

4 That's brilliant.

5 Keep going!

6 Be careful!

Keys to good practice
Communicating with children

✔ Use an appropriate method of communication for the child.

✔ Actively listen to the child.

✔ Encourage the child to develop ideas through speaking.

✔ Understand if children do not wish to communicate.

Promoting inclusion when working with children who have special educational needs

As an individual support assistant, you will need to work close to the child you are supporting to ensure that they have full access to the curriculum. This means that their needs make it difficult for them to manage without individual help in a mainstream classroom. There is a range of reasons why a child may have special needs.

The child's needs may be:

▷ **sensory or physical needs** which means that the child has difficulty due to limited mobility or has sensory needs such as blindness or deafness

▷ **emotional or behavioural needs** such as autism

▷ **specific learning difficulties** such as dyslexia which will mean that the child finds it hard to retain what they have learned

▷ **learning needs across the curriculum** which mean that children find all areas of learning difficult.

If you are employed to support an individual child, your line manager will usually be the SENCo or Special Educational Needs Co-ordinator. This member of staff, along with the class teacher, will be able to give you information and guidance about the work you will need to do with the child. Your job description should outline your responsibilities

---

Sandford Junior School
Job Description
Individual Support Assistant

Main purpose of the job

Be responsible for the care and welfare of the named child and assist the teacher in the education process.

Under the direction of the class teacher, to assist the pupil with his or her individual education programme.

Summary of responsibilities and personal duties

Duties may include any of the following

- Assist the pupil with his or her literacy programme, numeracy, motor skills or social skills programme(s).
- Assist in carrying out a modified curriculum.
- Where appropriate, act as an amanuensis (scribe) for the pupil.
- Prepare material, adapted by the class teacher, in order to give the pupil access to the curriculum.
- Assist the pupil to integrate and learn, usually within a group situation.
- Be responsible for the health and hygiene of the child including toileting and self care activities where necessary.
- Ensure that a pupil with medical needs is safe in physically demanding situations such as physical education or during school breaks.
- Ensure that the pupil remains focused and does not disrupt the classroom situation.
- Participate in the planning and implementation of the targets set in the child's Individual Education Plan.
- Where necessary, assist in the compilation of reports for use in assessment and annual reviews with other professionals.
- Report back either verbally and/or in writing on the child's performance.
- Undertake playground duties as necessary and accompany pupils on educational visits.
- Be prepared to liaise with other professionals and assist in implementing their advice.

▲ A job description for an individual support assistant

---

and what is expected of you as part of your role. There should be advice and help available to you and you should always ask for help if you need it.

You will need to be able to support these individual children in a variety of different situations and for different reasons. These may be for help with:

Different kinds of support	Where it is needed
Tasks where children have physical difficulties and need to have encouragement to help them to work safely and independently	Providing support for a child who cannot physically carry out tasks independently
Children who find it hard to pay attention and to keep on task	Encouraging children to re-focus on their work and encouraging them
Children who need to have an escort both inside and outside the school	Helping the child to think independently about what they need to do
Children whose challenging behaviour makes it difficult for others to learn	Helping them to achieve their behaviour targets

Your responsibilities for health, safety and security and child protection

Whilst working in a school environment, you will be responsible, along with other members of staff, for the health, safety and security of others. This means that you should be alert to any hazards which are likely to cause harm to yourself or others in the school. (you should also read Unit 3-10 Support the maintenance of pupil safety and security). Being alert to hazards includes not reporting them or taking no action when discovering a potential danger. Your job description should outline your responsibilities for health, safety and security within the school environment.

First Aid

You will also need to know what you should do if you are faced with situations where children need to have First Aid. The school will need to have at least one qualified First Aider who will be able to deal with minor injuries. If you find that you are working with or supervising children who need to have attention, you should always send for the First Aider whilst doing what you can, both to comfort them and to make sure that any injuries are dealt with to the best of your ability (Unit 3-10 covers what to do in case of more serious emergencies, Unit 3-11 page 206 has a section on minor illnesses).

You will often find yourself in situations where children are telling you that they have fallen over in the playground or are feeling unwell. As you get to know some children you may find that they are more likely to tell you about every small incident, whereas others may be hurt and say nothing. You should always take care to investigate, particularly when dealing with very young children. Some of them may be shy about talking to an adult or be too upset to do so.

▲ You will need to be responsible for the safety of pupils in the school environment

 Knowledge into action

If you have not done so already, ask if you can go out on playground duty alongside a teacher so that you can experience the kinds of situations described and find out how the teacher reacts.

Situations you may need to deal with
Bumps on the head – always record. Schools should have a place for this so the child should be sent to the first aider and monitor the child's progress.
Cuts and grazes – these should be washed in cold water by the first aider, unless they are very minor.
Aggression between children – if you are told about or have seen children hurting one another physically or verbally you will need to try to find out what has happened. If there is a long term problem with bullying you should always inform a more senior member of staff.
Sickness or soiling – if you are present when either of these situations occur, you should always send for another adult, usually by sending another child and keep other children away from the area. You may need to keep the child with you or send them to the toilet.
A child who is very upset – children can become very distressed, sometimes for a very minor reason, at other times because of something more serious. You may need to comfort them or sit with them until help arrives.
Bruising – if you notice that a child has more bruising than is likely you may need to report it to the class teacher so that it can be monitored, in case of child abuse.

Changes in behaviour you should report to others

You will need to look out for the kinds of behaviour patterns that may mean that there is something wrong with the child. If you notice a child behaving in a way that is out of character, you should always take it further. Either ask the child yourself if this is possible or report it to the class teacher, so that steps can be taken and parents informed if necessary. Children's behaviour can often be affected by issues which you might think of as minor or there may be a more complex problem. These can be called short-term or long-term factors.

Short-term factors – these are factors which may be short-lived but which have an influence on the child's learning and they may find it difficult to work as a result. Sometimes the situation may be one where all children are affected, for example before a Christmas party or when there is a visitor to the school.

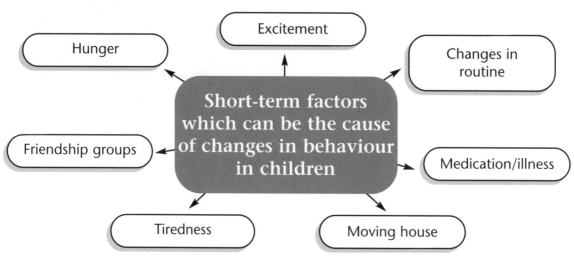

▲ Changes in behaviour can be affected by many factors

Long-term factors – these may also have a disruptive effect on the way in which children behave, but may be over a longer period of time:

Long-term factors can cause changes in behaviour
Divorce or separation of parents – the child may be angry with parents or find it hard to express how they feel. They may feel guilty and think that they are to blame and worried about what will happen next.
Physical abuse – children who are being abused may be nervous or jumpy around adults. They may be very quiet or withdrawn and lack self-esteem.
Sexual abuse – the child may have mood swings and changes in behaviour or display inappropriate behaviour.
Verbal abuse or bullying – a child who is being verbally abused or bullied may have poor self esteem and may repeat the abuse towards other children.
Bereavement – a child who has suffered a bereavement may be angry about what has happened and become detached from others.
Change in carer/adoption – this may have a disruptive influence on the child's home life and could affect their self-esteem as they may feel rejected. Children may become detached from others because of a fear of this happening again.

▲ Children will need support to enable them to learn

A child who is suffering through one of these long-term situations may display a variety of 'different' behaviours and you should look out for these and make sure that you report them to the class teacher. The child may need considerable support in school to help create a stable environment and enable their learning.

Legal and school requirements for child protection

The main requirements of child protection are within the Children Act 1989 and relate to putting the child's interests first. You should be aware of the school's policies and requirements when dealing with health, safety and security of pupils. This means that the school will have documented what it will do in order to protect children whilst in its care and you will need to use strategies which are used by the whole school.

School policies which may relate to children's emotional development may include:

▷ **Behaviour policy** – this will give staff strategies and guidelines when managing behaviour in school.

▷ **PSHEC policy** – this will give details of the way in which staff carry out the National Curriculum with regard to Personal, Social, Health and Citizenship Education.

▷ **Inclusion and equal opportunities policies** – these policies will promote the school's ethos and procedures in these two areas.

▷ **Anti-bullying policy** – since September 1999, schools have been legally required to implement anti-bullying policies.

▷ **Child protection policy** – this will effect the way staff are alerted at all times for signs of abuse or neglect in children. It will give you an indication of the key points that you need to observe and the person you need to go to in order to report any concerns.

You will need to know what kinds of strategies the school uses to diffuse and manage children's emotions. In your class, you may find that the class teacher uses different strategies for managing negative emotions. Circle time is often used in classrooms, although it is not always appropriate for very young children as they often need to sit for a long time to wait for their turn.

Knowledge into action

Ask if you can see a copy of your school's Child Protection Policy. What does it say about signs of abuse in children?

Evidence collection

Do a case study on a child who has shown unusual behaviour recently. You will need to find out about the child and exactly what has happened, for example whether they are reluctant to talk to others, reluctant to go to assembly, not eating their lunch or complaining of illness. Include lots of detail about the child and any situations on which you can gather information:

▶ How you could communicate with this child and support him or her?

▶ Would you report this to anyone?

▶ Would you go anywhere for further help?

Element 2-2.2 Help with the care and support of groups of pupils

For this element you will need to know and understand the following:

▶ how to work effectively with a group of pupils

▶ how to deal with conflicts and anti-social behaviour within groups.

How to work effectively with a group of pupils

For this element you will need to know and understand how to work with groups of children. You may find that you are often asked to work with groups, which may be organised in a variety of ways.

Different groups in the classroom
▶ Seating groups: pupils sit together but are engaged in separate tasks and produce separate outcomes, e.g. children who are working on the same maths activity may be working at their own pace, and will therefore achieve differently.
▶ Working groups: where pupils tackle similar tasks, which result in similar outcomes, but their work is independent, e.g. measuring different objects in the playground.
▶ Co-operative groups: where pupils have separate but related tasks which result in a joint outcome, e.g. a wall display of different paintings but all in the style of Monet.
▶ Collaborative groups: pupils have the same task and work together towards a joint outcome, e.g. a giant dragon for Chinese New Year.

Children will sometimes work very well together with little adult input, but you may find that you will need to help and guide some groups carefully so that they work effectively and achieve their learning outcomes – what they are expected to learn.

 Case study

You are working with Sally and Laurence's group on a PE activity. The children have been told that they are going to evaluate their dance activity, thinking about the different skills they were asked to apply. The children have started to discuss the evaluation but are arguing about it.

1 How could you help them to focus on what they are going to do?

2 What would you do if the group failed to carry out the task?

▲ Working with groups of children

Working in pairs

Two pupils who are working together should have a healthy exchange of ideas and give one another the opportunity to say what they think. If you are supervising them, you should make sure that they are both able to put their ideas forward and encourage them to do so by asking questions.

Where pupils are working together, they should be encouraged to say what they think without being worried about 'getting it wrong'. A child whose efforts are not recognised by an adult will be much less likely to put their forward their thoughts next time.

Groups of three or more

You will need to be interested and interact with each member of the group. It is important to remember that some members of the group may have more to say than others and will be more willing to put their ideas forward, whilst others may be quieter. Make sure that you encourage each member of the group to say what they are thinking so that they all have an equal opportunity.

Working with peers

It is not only small groups that need to work together; whole classes need to develop their own identity and work together as a class. Class teachers may tell you that some classes work very well together and bounce ideas off one another, whilst others find it more difficult due to personalities within the group!

Children may also be working with others from their class in a smaller group on the same concepts and ideas, for example in a subject such as maths and literacy. You may find that you need to help and encourage some children more than others. You should always reinforce positive interactions between pupils so that they are encouraged to co-operate with one another, for example, 'Look at how well Josie, Eric and Manuela are working on their measuring.' This will draw attention to what the others should be doing.

Knowledge into action

Observe the group dynamics in your class. Which children seem to work well together and why? Are there any clashes of personality? How does the class teacher group the children and why?

Working with younger pupils

Occasionally you may be asked to work with pupils who are younger or older than those you normally work with. It is always good for children to mix with others of different ages and work with them, as they will be encouraged to help and think about different groups of people.

Think about it

You are working with a group of Year 1 children who have just started to use the school library. They have been going on a weekly basis to familiarise themselves with the environment and have to be shown what to do before they are allowed to take books home. Some members of Year 6 have been given the responsibility of showing them how the system works and how to find different books. They have each been given a partner in the Year 1 class so that each week they know who they are helping and what they need to show them next.

▶ Do you think that this will be a good idea?

▶ Why might this system help both Year 1 and Year 6?

▶ What might you do to help and encourage both sets of children?

? Think about it

Look at these two conversations between an assistant and a group of children who are making a model of a boat:

A Nadeem: Do you think I should use this as a rudder? It will make the boat look more realistic.

Tom: Great! When we have put the sail on it's going to look really good.

Assistant: I think your boat needs a lot more work as it isn't going to float and a rudder is not what you need at the moment. You should forget about the rudder and concentrate on making it float.

B Nadeem: Do you think I should use this as a rudder? It will make the boat look more realistic.

Tom: Great! When we have put the sail on it's going to look really good.

Assistant: Well done, the rudder is a good idea. Why don't you finish the ideas you had in your design first and then you can move on to making changes.

▶ Which of these two assistants is more likely to motivate Nadeem to continue with his work?

▶ Why do you think that Nadeem might be unhappy with what the first assistant said?

▲ It is important to act as a role model for your pupils

Being a good role model

You will also need to show pupils that you always consider the needs and feelings of others. This means that at all times when you are in school, you should ensure that your behaviour towards children and other staff always shows respect and consideration. Pupils will always notice if you are telling them to do something and then not doing it yourself.

How to deal with conflicts and antisocial behaviour within groups

When children are working in groups, there will sometimes be areas of conflict between them. This could be due to a number of reasons shown below.

Pupils may find the task too difficult or too easy and start to lose interest as a result

In this situation you will not always be able to ask the class teacher for help. You may need to adapt the work the children have been given so that they are more able to focus on the task. You can do this by talking through what they have to do and simplifying it for them, or if it is too easy, finding a way of extending the children's ideas.

Pupils may be distracted by one another

This is the most common reason that groups break down. You will need to monitor the group's behaviour all the time to catch any inappropriate behaviour before it causes this to happen. As you get to know particular children, you will know that some children should not sit together or should not be together in the same group if they are to concentrate on their work.

 Think about it

You have been asked to work with a group of 4 Year 2 children on partitioning tens and units. The class teacher has asked you to sit with them and ensure that they understand the work they have been given as they have been through it on the previous day. However, the group find the task difficult and their behaviour begins to deteriorate as a result.

▶ How do you think you could get the group back to co-operating with one another without involving the class teacher?

▶ What other strategies could you use in this situation?

Ask your class teacher if you can observe him or her when working with a group of pupils. Look at whether the group are working together or individually. How does the teacher deal with any distractions amongst the group?

Pupils may find turn-taking and sharing difficult

This may be a problem, particularly with younger children who may all want to talk at once! This is something that some children need to be taught when they start school and some will always find it harder than others. You will need to talk through with them why it is important to let others have turns and why we should always consider the feelings of others.

One subject area which children learn about in schools is Personal, Social and Health Education or PSHE, which encourages children to think and talk about the feelings of others, as well as their own feelings. A way in which your school may do this is 'Circle Time', which encourages children to discuss issues in an open forum as a whole class.

Changes in routine may have had an effect on the children

This may be because children are working on something different, for example if they are together outside the school premises on a school trip. Situations such as this will always make children more excitable and you will need to be prepared for this. Children who have special educational needs and behavioural difficulties may also need to have extra preparation for changes in routine so that they know what is going to happen.

Pupils may display anti-social behaviour towards one another

This includes racist or sexist remarks, or comments that are unpleasant and abusive towards others. It is important that these kinds of anti-social behaviours are dealt with immediately so that children learn that they are not acceptable. If you find yourself in a situation where the behaviour of some members of the group is starting to affect the others you will always need to intervene. You may feel that you are unable to resolve some situations yourself – in cases like this you should always seek the assistance of other members of staff.

▲ School trips can make children more excitable

School policies when dealing with behaviour

Policies are written by teachers, governors and sometimes parents from guidelines which are given by the Local Education Authority (LEA). They will give information and guidance on how the school manages and deals with different areas, for example Health and Safety, Behaviour, Early Years and different curriculum areas such as Geography or Science. All parents should also have been given a prospectus or have a copy of a Home–School agreement which they should sign to indicate that they agree with the school's policies. They should also be revised and revisited by staff and governors on a regular basis.

Your school policy for behaviour will tell you how the school as a whole should work together to promote good behaviour and strategies the school uses to encourage this. It should also have a section on how the school deals with anti-social behaviour (you should also read Unit 3–1 page 143: Contribute to the management of pupil behaviour).

 Evidence collection

Simulation may be used to obtain evidence in relation to conflict situations and incidents of anti-social behaviour.

You are on duty in the playground when you find a group of children who are teasing and swearing at a girl who is on her own. You have asked them to leave her alone and come to another area of the playground but they challenge you and carry on upsetting the girl.

▶ Look at your school's policy for dealing with anti-social behaviour. What can/should you do?

▶ Discuss in your groups what you would do in this situation.

▶ As a group, write up a summary of the action that should be taken.

Keys to good practice
Managing groups

✔ Anticipate potential areas of conflict.

✔ Deal with any anti-social behaviour or refer to another member of staff if the situation is outside your role.

✔ Remember school policies when dealing with behaviour or conflict.

✔ Deal sensitively with issues surrounding bullying.

✔ Be a good role model.

✔ Be positive as far as possible.

End of unit test

1 How would you start to form positive relationships with individual pupils?

2 Name 2 ways you could encourage a child to be independent.

3 How could you show a child that you are actively listening to them?

4 What might a child with challenging behaviour need help with?

5 What does 'being a good role model' for children mean?

6 What kinds of groups might you find yourself working with?

7 Name 3 areas of conflict which may occur between groups.

8 Why will changes in routine have an effect on groups of children?

9 Look at these two statements:

▷ groups of children should always be made to work quietly

▷ children in groups will always be boisterous

Do you think that these statements are true or false? Why?

10 Where will you find information about what your school does when dealing with group behaviour?

References and further reading

Mosely, Jenny: *Quality Circle Time*

Kidscape – *How to stop bullying (for children 5–15)* Kidscape Tel: 0207 730 3300

Websites

www.dfes.gov.uk/bullying

www.bullying.co.uk

www.childline.org.uk

www.kidscape.org.uk

Unit 2-3 Provide support for learning activities

There are two elements to this unit. These are:

2-3.1 Support the teacher in the planning and evaluation of learning activities
2-3.2 Support the delivery of learning activities

This unit explores the kind of support that you should provide to the teacher in order to ensure pupils' effective teaching and learning. It will help you to provide support in planning and giving feedback to the teacher about learning activities within the class. This will include sharing any concerns with the teacher about the timing, groups or nature of the support you are asked to give.

When you are supporting the delivery of learning activities, you will need to carry out the work with the children as agreed, using the appropriate materials and support. You will need to make sure that you monitor the learning activities and if necessary break down or extend the pupil's work. You should then evaluate the learning activities and report back to the teacher.

Element 2-3.1 Support the teacher in the planning and evaluation of learning activities

For this element, you will need to know and understand the following:

▶ the relationship between your role and the role of the teacher within the learning environment

▶ your role and responsibilities for supporting pupils' learning

▶ planning and evaluation of learning activities

▶ how and when to provide feedback on the activity to the teacher: evaluating learning activities.

The relationship between your role and the role of the teacher within the learning environment

When you are supporting children, you will need to be clear about your role and what you are expected to do, so that you can carry out your duties effectively. (you should also see Unit 2-1 page 3) It is important that you know exactly what these are, what the teacher is expecting of you and what the children should achieve from each activity. For this reason, you should have a clear idea about what you are doing during each session both through planning with the teacher and through your own experience in the classroom. The main differences between your two roles are shown below, although as you can see the two roles should complement one another.

Some of the duties of a teacher and those of a teaching assistant	
Teachers' role*	**Teaching assistant's role**
To be responsible for planning and preparing the National (or Foundation) Curriculum	To plan and prepare work alongside the teacher
To teach pupils according to their educational needs	To carry out learning activities effectively as directed by the teacher
To assess, record and report on the development, progress and attainment of pupils	To assess/evaluate children's work as directed by the teacher
To take responsibility for all other adults within the classroom (assistants, volunteer helpers)	To report any problems or queries to the teacher
To communicate and consult with the parents of pupils	To give feedback to the teacher following planned activities
To communicate and co-operate with persons or bodies outside the school	
To participate in meetings arranged for any of the above purposes	
Teachers will also usually be responsible for managing an area of the curriculum, such as Maths and this will be included in their job description.	
*Source: from School Teachers' Pay and Conditions Document	

As you can see, the main part of your role is being guided and led by the teacher with regard to the work you carry out with the children. You will need to be able to work with the teacher and activities should be carefully planned together. The kinds of activities that you plan with the teacher may be as single lessons or could be a series of lessons relating to a particular subject area.

Individual support assistants

If you are an individual support assistant rather than a classroom assistant and are working with one particular child, you may find that your role is slightly different, although there will be some areas that overlap. The main differences are that an individual support assistant will focus time on a specific child, and may be less involved in planning and evaluating class activities (more on this on page 56).

How the responsibilities of classroom assistants and individual support assistants may differ	
Classroom assistant	**Individual support assistant**
Duties may include:	**Duties may include:**
Assisting teacher with classroom organisation Attending planning meetings	Developing an understanding of the specific needs of the child
Preparing resources	To assist the class teacher with the development of an individual programme of support
Supervising individual children or groups	To help the child to learn effectively

Objectives of learning activities

When you are planning or working with individual children or groups, you will need to know the learning objective – that is, what the children are expected to learn from the activity. In Reception, you will be working towards the Early Learning Goals at the end of the Foundation Stage. In Years 1–6, the learning objectives will be based on what children need to be taught from the National curriculum. You will be expected to work with the children to ensure that the learning objectives have been achieved. If they are not able to achieve the learning objective, you must inform the class teacher when you give feedback on the work you have done with the children.

 Think about it

Are you always clear about learning objectives when you are carrying out work with children? Make sure that you always ask the teacher. Think to yourself every time – 'What are the children going to learn from this?'

Other requirements of your role

You will also have the opportunity to carry out other duties within the classroom which give support to the class and the teacher in more practical ways, such as ensuring that all the required resources are available. (see also page 5 Unit 2-1). If you find that you are often 'in between' activities and the whole class is listening to the teacher or working without support, you will need to be able to plan for yourself the kinds of tasks you could be doing. It is important that you use your time effectively so that you are not waiting to be 'told' what to do next. The following kinds of activities will always need doing in a busy classroom and you should be aware of them.

> ▶ Sharpening pencils ▶ Filing work ▶ Putting up and taking down displays ▶ Mounting work to be displayed ▶ Collecting or replacing resources from the appropriate place ▶ Tidying areas within the classroom ▶ Labelling ▶ Filling in assessment forms ▶ Preparing children's books or folders ▶ Setting up activities such as computers, televisions, roamers and other ICT equipment

▲ Activities to be done in a busy classroom

Think about it

Ask your line manager if you and your colleagues can make a list of duties you may be expected to perform. Ask the class teachers in the school if they can also list what they expect teaching assistants to do. It may be an interesting exercise to see whether these two lists differ in any way. How do the kinds of duties listed relate to your job description?

Your role and responsibilities for supporting pupils' learning

You will need to be sure exactly how you are required to support children and this should be made clear when you plan activities with the teacher. This is because if you are working with a group of children on an activity and the teacher is busy in another part of the classroom, you will not be able to ask questions during the activity. It is important that you are aware of exactly what you are doing and how to deal with children who finish early or are having difficulties (see element 2-3.2 for ideas about help with this) If you have ideas of your own about the kinds of things you could do when supporting children, you should have the opportunity to suggest these to the teacher at the planning stage. If you are able to see potential difficulties within the activities, you should also point them out if possible to the class teacher.

Supporting children with Special Educational Needs

As already discussed in Units 2-1 and 2-2, children who have special educational needs will need to have their work differentiated (planning different work for children's abilities) so that they are able to access the curriculum. If you are going to be working with a child with special needs, you will have to find out exactly what their needs are. You should be able to find out through speaking to the class teacher or SENCo and looking at the child's Statement. You will also need to look at Unit 2-2 on supporting individual children for what inclusion means and how it will affect your role. At the time of writing, schools should also have written or be developing their own Inclusion Policy.

When you are working with children who have special needs you may need to have additional training depending on their condition and/or the kinds of activities you may need to work on with them. For example, a child who is visually impaired may need to have one-to-one support with PE.

Planning and evaluation of learning activities

Many activities which children undertake each week within the classroom will be timetabled. Before you start thinking about planning you will need to have a classroom timetable so that you can see when different subject areas need to be planned for and at what times. For children in Reception, the Foundation stage curriculum will mean that children do not all work on the same subject at the same time within the classroom until towards the end of the year. However, between Years 1 and 6, children will work on the Literacy and Numeracy strategies together and will usually have more subject-based lessons, although work will need to be differentiated to take account of children's abilities.

Timetables show when different subjects are to take place.									
	9.00	9.10	9.30	10.30	10.50	11.35	12.00	1.15	2.15
Mon	Registration	Assembly	Literacy hour	Playtime	Numeracy	Music	Lunch/ playtime	Computer suite	TV and follow up
Tue	Registration	Assembly	Hall time	Playtime	Numeracy	RE	Lunch/ playtime	Literacy	Library time
Wed	Registration	Assembly	Literacy hour	Playtime	Numeracy	Circle time	Lunch/ playtime	Swimming (all afternoon)	
Thur	Registration	Assembly	Literacy hour	Playtime	Numeracy	Spelling Test	Lunch/ playtime	History (topic work)/Art	Art/history
Fri	Registration	Assembly	Literacy hour	Playtime	Numeracy	Quiet reading time	Lunch/ playtime	Geography	PE

▲ Teachers and assistants will need to have time to plan and discuss activities together

Why do we use planning and evaluation?

Planning and evaluation are very important as they enable us to see what children have achieved and how we can take them further next time. We need to find out what children know so that we can teach them the next stage.

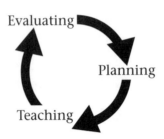

Plans will need to take account each child's abilities and should show how different children are catered for within the class.

For an example of how different abilities are catered for within a maths activity, see page 137.

Long, medium and short term planning

You will also need to know about the different kinds of plans used in schools. Usually, teachers plan for the **long term** (over a term or half term), then the **medium term** (over a week) and finally **short term** (for the day). You should have a copy of the long term plan if you are working with a particular class, so that you have some idea of the kinds of topics you will be working on with the children. Medium term plans may be worked on at the start or before the start of the term so that staff know in which order and which week topics are going to be covered. It is also important to know when different resources will be needed and how classes will ensure that they are accessible to all.

 Think about it

Class 4G are doing some project work on the human body. They are in a three-form entry school and all three classes will need to use the school's resources (x-ray pictures, books) during week 3 of the term. Discuss in your groups how you think the school could ensure that all classes will be able to have access to the resources.

Planning with the class teacher

Planning may work in one of two ways. You may have time set aside to plan with the teacher, or the teacher may devise the plan and then work through it with you to ensure that you are happy with the activities you are asked to do and if you have anything to add. Through your own experience in the learning environment, you may find that you have your own suggestions or ideas. Plans will also need to be accessible to all those who are working with the class, for example students or individual support assistants, so that they also have a clear understanding of what is going to happen.

Through planning with the teacher, you will be able to consider the activities you are going to work on with children and make preparations. For example, if you are going to work the next day with a group of children on finding materials which may be suitable for making cuddly toys, you may like to bring in some materials from home or think about variations which you could use.

 Knowledge into action

Next time you are planning with the class teacher, note down any queries or questions you ask at this stage. Can you forsee any problems?

All plans need to include details of what all adults are expected to do and there should also be a space for assessment and follow-up, which the teacher will usually fill in. However, if you have carried out a learning activity with the children, you will need to make sure you pass on information about the activity to help with assessment (see also page 75). There should also be a space on Foundation Stage plans for the teacher to write on the Stepping Stones towards the Early Learning Goals, so that it is clear what the children are going to learn from each activity (see page 60).

You may not always be shown the teacher's plans – for reasons of time you may be told verbally what you are going to be doing. This may mean that you will need to write things down so that you remember what you are doing and the kind of preparations you will need to make. As you become more experienced, you will find that you become quicker at thinking of the kinds of things you will need for an activity.

 Case study

Jai has been asked to work with a group of Year 1 children the following day on looking at how they have changed since they were babies. She has been asked to discuss with the children what they think they can do now that they could not do before and to record using a simple 'then and now' sheet.

1 How do you think Jai could make the activity more interesting for the children?

2 What kinds of preparations might Jai make before starting the activity?

Monday		Early Learning Goals*
9–9.15:	Register/showing time.	
9.15–9.30:	Sharing 'Goldilocks' big book with the class. Look at and discuss cover. Find out what the children think the book will be about. Where is the title of the book, the author? TA - set up painting activity.	(C, L & L – Sustain attentive listening, responding to what they have heard by relevant comments, questions or actions.) (C, L & L – Interact with others, negotiating plans and activities and taking turns in conversation.)
	• 9.30–10.10: TA taking groups to paint • CT working with a group on sequencing Goldilocks story • Construction: children to make a home for a bear • Sand: using small bears – make a den for a bear • Role play area – 3 bears' house • Listening corner – tapes of bear stories	(C.Dvt – use their imagination in art and design . . .) (M.Dvt – sequencing is a stepping stone rather than an early learning goal) (K & U – build and construct with a wide range of objects . . .) (C, L & L – Use language to imagine and recreate roles and experiences) (C, L & L – Listen with enjoyment and respond to stories, songs and music . . .)
10.10:	Whole class to work on phonics CT teaching new sound – 'w' TA to write in phonic books ready for children. All to write new sound. Learn sound and watch letter formation.	(C, L & L – Link sounds to letters, naming and sounding the letters of the alphabet)
10.30:	Playtime	
10.45:	Milk and story	
11.00:	Continue with groups from this morning.	
11.40:	Music – loud and soft. Children in circle. Think about the different voices we use in school. Playground voice, classroom voice, singing voice.	(C.Dvt – Recognise and explore how sounds can be changed . . .)
12.00:	Lunch/playtime	
1.15:	Register, assembly.	(PSE – Maintain attention, concentration and sit quietly when appropriate)
1.45:	Parent in to listen to children read. Maths afternoon: starting with mental maths – counting and finding 'one more than' • Puzzles • Making patterns with beads and recording • Computer – counting and sorting program • CT working with groups on practical addition • TA assessing number formation	(M.Dvt – Recognise numerals 1 to 9 begin to relate addition to combining two groups of objects . . . talk about, recognise and recreate simple patterns using developing mathematical ideas and methods to solve practical problems use language such as more and less to compare two numbers) (M.Dvt – Counting and recognising numbers, say number names in familiar contexts . . .) (C, L & L – Listen with enjoyment and respond to stories . . .)
2.45:	Television – number programme	
3.00:	Storytime	
3.15:	Home	

* Six areas of learning:
Communication, Language and Literacy; Mathematical Development; Knowledge and Understanding of the World; Physical Development; Creative Development; Personal, Social and Emotional Development

▲ An example of a short-term plan which may be used in a Reception class of 26 children

Potential difficulties with planning

If the plans include supporting children in activities where you feel that you need to have more training, you should always point these out to the class teacher. You will always need to ensure that you feel comfortable with what you are carrying out so that you can confidently support the children. Teaching assistants are increasingly being asked to support tasks within the Literacy and Numeracy strategies, for example and you should ask for training if it is not automatically offered to you. (see unit 2–5 for more on Literacy and Numeracy.)

You will need to make sure that you have enough time for planning, particularly if you are not experienced and are likely to have more questions. If your class teacher does not seem aware of this, you should ask him or her, or failing this you should mention it to your mentor or supervisor. It is important that you feel confident about what you are doing.

Sometimes in schools changes will need to be made to plans, perhaps as a result of something unexpected happening such as a change in planned activities. This is unavoidable and you will need to be flexible enough to be able to manage these kinds of situations. When children have changes to their routine, their behaviour may be affected and you will also need to take this into consideration. (see also page 151)

▲ You will need to have training when working on literacy and numeracy activities

Case study

It is PE week in school. You have planned to do a maths activity with a group of children but the children are getting very excited about a visitor who is coming later that day to demonstrate circus skills. Although the activity starts off well, one of the children mentions the circus and the group's excitement is starting to prevent them from working.

1 What would you do in this situation?

2 Could you continue to work if the group continued to behave in this way?

How to provide feedback to the teacher: evaluating learning activities

As well as planning with the class teacher, you will also need to be able to help with evaluation. This means that you should be able to give feedback to the teacher on how particular sessions have worked with children and whether they have achieved their learning objectives. You may also give suggestions for how you think they may be improved next time. You may do this verbally or be asked to fill in evaluation sheets which will ask for specific details and be kept for record-keeping purposes. If the feedback is verbal, you will need to make sure that you have time with the class teacher so that you can pass on all the relevant information.

Lesson evaluation

▷ Sometimes it may be easier to evaluate by exception – that is, to record that all children have achieved the learning objective except those whose names you have taken down.

▷ You will also need to say how different children responded to the activity and tell the teacher about any assessments you have carried out.

Subject	Learning objective	Date of activity	Comments
Science	Understanding of pushes and pulls	14th February	Donna's group found the activity easy. Both Jack and Shaun's groups worked through successfully. Selina needed lots of help. Next time, try more discussion first.

▲ Example of an evaluation sheet

▷ If any of the materials used have caused a problem or resources have not worked properly this will need to be mentioned.

▷ If you find that you do not have enough time to carry out the activity properly, this will need to be reported to the class teacher, so that additional time can be allowed for the next time.

 Case study

Sarah has been working with a group of children on map skills. The children have had to locate different places on a map and show that they understand the different items on the key. She has been asked to assess whether the children have achieved the learning objective of 'understanding the use of a key' and write any comments. However, Sarah has not been able to complete the activity and feels that some of the children would have done better if they had been given longer.

1 Should Sarah say anything to the class teacher?

2 Do you think Sarah should repeat the activity with any of the children?

▲ You will need to make sure you speak to the teacher about learning activities at an appropriate moment.

▷ If you need to tell the teacher about a problem that has occurred while you are supporting children, always ensure that you choose an appropriate moment to discuss it. For example, it would not be sensible to try and speak to the teacher whilst others are present or if children are also trying to attract his or her attention.

Keys to good practice
Planning and evaluation

✔ Make sure you have time set aside for planning.

✔ Ensure you understand what you have been asked to do and are aware of learning objectives.

✔ Point out any queries you have or potential difficulties at the planning stage.

✔ Make sure you understand any differentiated activities.

✔ Ensure there is time for evaluation at the end of the task.

Evidence collection

Carry out an activity in the classroom which you have planned alongside the teacher.

Ensure that you note down exactly what you are required to do, including the learning objectives, any special needs requirements, and any difficulties you anticipate which may change the way you carry out the activity.

Show how and when you provided feedback and evaluation of the activity to the class teacher.

Element 2-3.2 Support the delivery of learning activities

For this element, you will need to know and understand the following:

▶ principles underlying pupils' development and learning

▶ how to use praise, commentary and assistance

▶ how to monitor pupils' response to the learning activities and provide follow-up support.

How children learn and develop

There has been a great deal of research by educationalists and psychologists into the ways in which children learn and are influenced as they develop. There are also other, inbuilt influences on children's learning which will be discussed on page 67, as they will also have a direct effect on how children learn. The two main theories about how children's learning takes place are called behaviourist theory and cognitive theory. By looking at these we are able to think about different aspects of children's learning and consider how to best support them in school.

Behaviourist theory

This theory was first put forward by B.F Skinner (1904–1994). Skinner's theory is that as individuals we will repeat experiences which are enjoyable and avoid those which are not. This is as relevant for learning experiences as for behaviour itself. For example, a child who learns that it is enjoyable to work with construction toys will want to repeat the experience and do this again. If they are praised for working at a particular task, this may also reinforce their desire to repeat the experience. Skinner stated that good experiences were called *positive reinforcement*. Many educationalists use the strategy of positive reinforcement when working with children, for example by praising and encouraging them and by giving them tasks at which they can succeed.

How to promote positive reinforcement

We can ensure that children are gaining positive experiences when working by giving them:

▷ praise and encouragement

▷ enjoyable tasks

▷ manageable tasks.

Assistants will need to be aware of children's reactions to tasks as sometimes children may find it difficult to become motivated and lose enthusiasm quickly. It is important to recognise when children are not enjoying tasks and find out what may be the cause, so that we can encourage and motivate them. As assistants get to know children, it will be more apparent when they are not 'themselves', or able to focus on what they are

▲ Adults will need to be aware when children are not able to focus on a task

doing. Where children are not responding to a task, assistants should talk to them individually and try to find out the cause. There may be a variety of reasons why the child is not motivated:

▷ the child does not understand the requirements of the task
▷ the child is unable to complete the task as it is too difficult
▷ the child finds the task too easy
▷ there may be individual reasons why the child is not able to focus on the task, such as illness or anxiety.

Case study

Mike is working as a teaching assistant in a Year 5 class. Although he is working with a group on an art activity he has noticed that Connor, on the other side of the classroom, looks very unhappy and is not doing his work.

1 What should Mike do first?
2 Could he leave his group and go and talk to Connor?

Once the cause has been established, assistants may need to work closely with the child or speak to the teacher about the problem to decide the best way to work with the child. Where the task is too easy or too difficult, it may be possible to put the child with another group of children and restructure their work for later. Children whose work is not enjoyable or manageable will be unlikely to want to repeat the experience.

Cognitive Development Theory

The second theory of learning is that which was put forward by Jean Piaget, (1896–1980) and is based on the cognitive model. This states that a child will need to pass through different stages of a learning process. He stated that children pass through stages of learning which are broadly related to their age and that they cannot move from one stage to another until they are ready.

Types of learning		
Age	**Stage of learning**	**Characteristics**
0–2 yrs	Sensory motor stage	Babies are starting to find out about the world around them and are discovering what things around them can do.
2–6 yrs	Pre-operational stage	Children are starting to develop thought processes and are using symbolic play. They find it easier to learn when they can see and use practical examples.
6–11 yrs	Concrete operations stage	Children are able to think on a more abstract level. They can use more abstract concepts, for example a box can represent a car.

This theory has been criticised as all children learn and develop at a different pace and it is hard to say at exactly what age particular skills will develop. It is accepted however that children have individual learning needs and requirements.

 Think about it

Think about the children in your class and compare them with the table above. Do you think that children broadly speaking will pass through these stages at the suggested ages?

Factors which influence children's learning

Children's learning is not only influenced by their stage of development. There are also a number of individual factors which will affect each child when it comes to their learning. These are based on their own experiences and personality so will be different for each child. An assistant will need to consider these factors when supporting children in order to understand each child's needs.

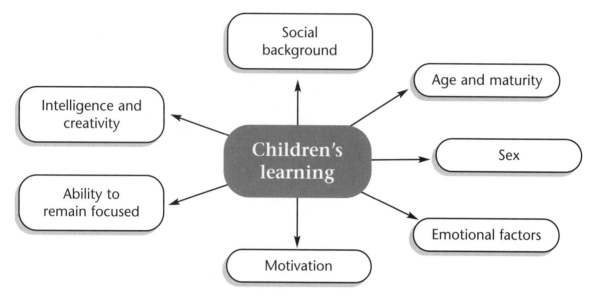

▲ Individual factors will affect each child's learning

▷ **Intelligence and creativity** – each child will have his or her own talents and aptitudes, so will be more or less able at different tasks within the classroom. They may also perceive themselves to be better or worse than other children and this may affect their motivation. For example, if they notice that another child is particularly good at a creative task such as art, they may think that their own work is not as good and feel inadequate. The adult will need to speak to and encourage the child so that they are able to continue. As children will always have strengths and weaknesses in different areas, the role of the adult will be to encourage children and instil awareness that all of us are different and that this is a positive thing.

 Case study

Robert is in Reception and is quite immature for his age. He has difficulty staying focused and holding his pencil and is reluctant to record anything, although he is able to talk about his ideas. He has started to notice that some of the other children do not find recording as difficult as he does. When it comes to writing his letter sounds with you one day, Robert says that he doesn't want to because it is too hard.

1 What would you say to Robert?

2 How could you help him to develop his confidence?

▷ **Social background** – children's background will have an influence on their learning as they may come to school with a variety of experiences. Some children may have had a wide range of social interactions, whilst others may have had very little. Where children's experiences are limited, they may lack confidence with others, find the setting difficult to adjust to or take longer to relate to other adults. This may affect their learning. They will need encouragement and praise to develop their confidence and skills when dealing with others.

▷ **Age and maturity** – as we have already seen, children will develop at an individual pace and so in any group of children there will be some who are more mature than others. Also, due to the way in which some schools have their intakes, there may be children in the same class or group who are a year or more apart in age. At an early age, this may make a big difference to the range of abilities which exist in the class. Adults should therefore be aware of this factor when monitoring children's learning.

▷ **Motivation** – this will directly affect the child's learning as it is the child's desire to learn and the interest which they have in a task. Where a child is not interested, does not see the purpose, or is unable to do a task, he or she may quickly become de-motivated. The adult should therefore be aware of this and make sure that the task is at the right level, is enjoyable, and makes sense to the child.

▷ **Emotional factors** – naturally, children will be affected by whether their home life is happy and settled. A child may have been living with parents who are going

▲ Mixed-age classes will have children with a wider than usual range of abilities

though a divorce or a child may have been bereaved. Sometimes they may be deeply affected by something seemingly insignificant to an adult, such as not saying goodbye to their mother that morning or having an argument with a sibling. Any of these things may have an impact on the child's ability to learn. You may need to take them away from the situation and talk to them to find out what is upsetting them and give them reassurance before attempting to continue. If the child is too upset to work, the best thing to do is remove them from the situation and try again later when they are feeling better.

Case study

Hannah's parents have just separated and she has missed 2 weeks of school while her mother finds somewhere else to live. When Hannah comes back, she is very clingy and emotional and unable to concentrate on her work.

1 How do you think you could support Hannah at this time?

2 What could you do if she is unable to do her work?

3 Is there anything you could do if this continued for a long period?

▷ **Sex** – the sex of a child may affect their learning, particularly if they have been given greater or fewer opportunities owing to their gender. It is important that we do not favour boys or girls in school when directing questioning and do not have expectations of one sex over another. For example, research shows that girls are generally quicker to read, but this could be due to the expectations of adults (more on this on page 164).

▷ **Ability to concentrate** – children of different ages will vary in their ability to concentrate on tasks and to sit and listen when required, although children of the same age may have a similar concentration span. Teachers should be aware of the length of time the children in their class are able to focus on a task, so that the work given or the amount of time they are required to sit still is not too demanding for them. Where one child's ability to concentrate is markedly different from that of his or her classmates, this may affect the learning of both the individual and of the rest of the class.

Length of concentration expected of children at different stages of development

0–2 years: children are unable to concentrate for long on one activity and will copy adults and other children. They are easily distracted from what they are doing.

2–3 years: children will start to be able to concentrate for short periods although they will find waiting difficult. They may start to play alongside other children.

3–5 years: children will be able to sit and share a story for a short time. They will start to take turns and play more co-operatively with others.

5–8 years: children will start to be able to work independently for short periods depending on their maturity and ability.

8–11 years: children should be able to focus on a task for a given time without distractions. They will be able to work on activities that require them to read instructions and carry out set tasks.

Strategies to support children's learning

A pupil who is not focused on the adult or the task may:

▷ start to disturb other children
▷ be distracted and fidgety
▷ misbehave and try to gain attention
▷ start daydreaming.

Where pupils are not concentrating on a given task, you must ensure that you try to involve them again as soon as possible. You can do this by:

▷ removing any distractions to refocus the child's attention on what they are doing
▷ giving praise where possible to give them encouragement
▷ making yourself available and approachable so that children are able to ask you for help if they are finding an activity challenging. You can do this by staying close to children who you know may find the work hard so that they can ask for help if they need it.
▷ being able to manage spontaneous opportunities which may arise when children are working such as commenting on things which the children are finding out, pointing out any funny coincidences and so on.
▷ varying the pace of learning if pupils are finding a task too easy or too difficult. You may need to backtrack, to ensure children understand the task or find ways of extending the task if they complete it quickly.

Think about it

Ask if you can observe the teacher working with a group of children. Look at the way in which he or she uses the above strategies to keep the children on task. Which do you think are the most effective?

How to use praise, commentary and assistance

All adults within the classroom will need to give children encouragement through praise, commentary and assistance. It is important for you to know how to give these to children although you may find that you do it automatically without realising!

Effective use of praise during learning activities

As you will be working with children who are learning all the time, it is vital that you use praise and encouragement to keep them on task and motivate them in their learning. This kind of reward is very effective, although it must be clear to children why they are being praised. It is important as you get to know children to praise their efforts as well as their achievements. This means that if they try their best at a task, it is important that adults notice and give them some encouragement. They will need to have recognition for what they do and this could take several forms:

▷ tell them that they are doing well

▷ comment on specific work that they are doing, for example 'You are working really hard on those co-ordinates, Trevor'

▷ ask them to show the teacher or another adult at an appropriate time to gain additional approval

▷ give them merit/house points or other reward systems used by the school.

You should also be aware of school policies for praise and rewards, so that you know the kinds of systems which the school uses. (see also Unit 3.1 page 158 on behaviour)

Knowledge into action

Observe a group of children who have been asked to work on the same task. How long do different children in the group remain focused on the activity? Is there much difference between the children – does anyone disturb the others or ask them to be quiet?

Think about it

Philip has been working on a close observational drawing of a model boat. He finds art activities challenging but has taken his time and is producing a very impressive piece of work. You notice that Philip is starting to look around at his friends and is losing his concentration.

1 What could you do to keep Philip on task?

2 How could you encourage him to complete his work?

▲ Children may become easily distracted if they are not able to complete the task

Commentary

This means helping children by talking them through what they have been asked to do. Sometimes children find it difficult to respond to instructions, have not heard clearly or are unable to remember exactly what they need to do. You can do this in several ways:

1 **Ask children what they think they need to do:** this is always a good starting point as you will find out straight away which children have taken on board what the teacher has said. In this way you will ensure that you have the right starting point for your work with the children.

2 **Repeat back what the teacher has said:** You may need to help children by repeating the instructions back to them if they are not clear about a task.

3 **Demonstrate what they need to do:** this may help some children who have not understood the requirements of the task. If it is a practical activity, you may need to have the final product to hand to show the children what it could look like when they have finished!

4 **Talk them through the process:** this may help some children and helps to reinforce their understanding of the learning objectives.

Case study

You are working with Vicky who has had 'glue ear' and is having some difficulty hearing what is happening in class. She has been asked to work through an exercise to fill in the correct use of 'there' and 'their.' However it becomes clear straight away that Vicky is unsure of what to do.

1 How could you help Vicky?

2 What would you say to the teacher at the end of the day?

Remember – many children suffer from colds and ear infections which will intermittently limit their ability to hear in class.

Assistance

This may be a difficult area for assistants because you may not be clear about how much help to give children when they are finding their work hard to complete. Children should always be encouraged to try to find their own solutions to tasks, but there will be times when they lose their enthusiasm because the task seems too difficult for them. In this situation, you will need to work through a checklist before telling the teacher:

▲ You may need to help a child by explaining what the task involves

▷ make sure the child has understood the concept covered by the teacher – you may need to go over this again with them (for example when to use commas or how to add fractions together)

▷ go over the requirements of what they have been asked to do

▷ ensure that there are no other reasons that they may not be able to focus on the task (for example an upset at home or between friends)

▷ break down the task so that it does not seem so daunting, for example 'Now try and do the first two and see how you get on and I will come back and see how you are doing'.

How to monitor pupils' response to the learning activities and provide follow-up support

In order to fully support pupils, you will need to look carefully at how they respond to the learning activities you have been asked to do with them. Ideally, the task will be set at exactly the right level and the child will complete it independently and without distractions and fulfil the learning objectives. However, this will not always happen and you will need to know what to do. Children may respond to learning activities in different ways:

▷ **The activity may be too difficult** – when children start work on an activity always look round to make sure they are all attempting to do it. You will be able to tell if a child is finding an activity too difficult as they will usually look 'lost', unhappy or distracted. You may need to help them in this instance – this might mean showing them exactly what to do and giving them further examples. If the task is still too difficult, you may need to simplify it if possible.

Think about it

Rory is a Year 2 child working on a symmetry activity involving shapes and has to draw reflections. He is able to reproduce regular shapes as reflections but is finding irregular ones much harder and is starting to become frustrated.

▶ How would you go about supporting Rory?

▶ What could you do if he was still unable to complete the task?

▷ **The task is not challenging enough for the pupil** – the pupil may complete the task easily and quickly and ask you what they should do next. You may not be able to ask the teacher and might need to give the child a further challenge by either extending the activity or by directing them to another activity within the classroom.

▷ **The child may not be confident enough to approach the task** – sometimes children have low self esteem and do not think that they are able to complete a task when they may be able to with a little encouragement and support. You may need to give the child some help to get them started.

Think about it

Christopher has been asked to do some writing about his school trip. He looks at the blank page for a while and when you ask him if he is still thinking about what he wants to say he tells you, 'I can't do this Miss – I'm rubbish at writing.'

▶ What could you say to encourage Christopher?

▶ Would you do anything else to encourage him once he had completed the task?

▷ **The child may misbehave or refuse to do the activity** – you may find that a child refuses to carry out the activity. This may be challenging and you may need to remove them from the situation to avoid distracting other children. If a child persistently refuses to settle to the learning activity you will need to speak to the class teacher straight away.

Other distractions

Pupils may be unable to complete the activity for other reasons such as lack of time or outside influences such as noise, illness or anxiety. In this case you will need to help them by either moving to a more comfortable area or abandoning the activity until another time.

Keys to good practice
Supporting children during learning activities

✔ Ensure both you and the children understand what you are required to do.

✔ Use a range of questioning strategies.

✔ Make sure you listen to all the children.

✔ Reassure children who are less confident about their ideas.

✔ Give positive praise wherever possible.

✔ Adapt work where necessary.

✔ Inform the teacher of any problems which have taken place.

✔ Provide a level of assistance which allows children to achieve without helping them too much.

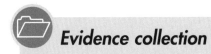

Evidence collection

Ask the class teacher if you can carry out an activity with a group of children. Make sure that you carefully monitor each child's response to the activity and note down whether they are able to fulfil the learning objective. Record both the childrens' responses and how you used different strategies to support them during the activity.

End of unit test

1 Name 2 ways in which your role and the role of the teacher are different.

2 What is the main difference between an Individual Support Assistant and a Teaching assistant?

3 What can you do at the planning stage to help the teacher?

4 What is differentiation?

5 Name the 3 types of planning to be found in schools.

6 Why is it important to evaluate learning activities?

7 How might you find out about the needs of an SEN child you are supporting?

8 Name 2 ways in which you can ensure that children have positive experiences when working.

9 What kinds of factors will have an influence on children's learning?

10 How would you keep a child on task if they are becoming distracted?

References

Schoolteachers' pay and conditions document (DFES, 2002)

National Numeracy Strategy (DFES)

National Literacy Strategy (DFES)

Curriculum Guidance for the Foundation Stage (QCA,2000)

Websites

www.qca.org.uk

www.lg-employers.gov.uk: look under the A–Z subject listing for the National Occupational Standards for Teaching and Classroom Assistants and further details about the NVQ.

Unit 2-4 Provide effective support for your colleagues

There are two elements to this unit. These are:

2-4.1 Maintain working relationships with colleagues
2-4.2 Develop your effectiveness in a support role

This unit will show you how you can maintain effective working relationships with your colleagues which are consistent with your job role. You will need to show that you can deal with any difficulties you have through using your own initiative where possible or through approaching those who have the authority to deal with them. You will also need to make sure that you understand legal and ethical requirements for issues such as confidentiality of information.

When you are developing your own effectiveness in relation to your role, you will need to show that you understand the expectations of your job. You should always seek feedback from others as to how you are fulfilling these expectations and work towards identifying areas for development.

Element 2-4.1 Maintain working relationships with colleagues

For this element, you will need to know and understand the following:

▶ your role and how it relates to the role of others in the school
▶ the lines and methods of communication that apply within the school setting
▶ principles underlying effective communication skills and how these may be applied within the school environment
▶ school policies for dealing with difficulties in working relationships and practices.

Your role and how it relates to the role of others within the school

In Unit 2-3, you were able to look at how your role and the role of the teacher complement one another within the learning environment. However, classroom teachers and assistants are part of a wider picture within the school. You will need to be aware of how all members of staff fit together so that you can build up a picture of how they work as a team.

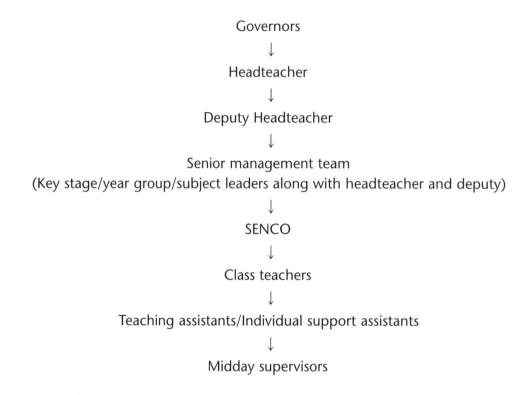

Governors
↓
Headteacher
↓
Deputy Headteacher
↓
Senior management team
(Key stage/year group/subject leaders along with headteacher and deputy)
↓
SENCO
↓
Class teachers
↓
Teaching assistants/Individual support assistants
↓
Midday supervisors

▲ Example of the management system within an infant school

It may be that within this system, the Deputy headteacher is also a year group or Key Stage manager, who has responsibility for a group of teachers. If the school has only one form entry, there will be no need for a year group leader, but there should be a manager for each Key Stage, including an Early Years manager for the Foundation stage. It is very important in all schools that all members of staff are valued and that lines of communication are always open, through formal and informal opportunities for discussion. (see page 88 – 'How information is passed through the school')

On a daily basis you will probably work most closely with:

▷ class teachers

▷ other assistants

▷ other adults within the school. These may be voluntary helpers such as parents or employed, for example caretakers, computer technicians, office staff, midday supervisors

▷ outside agencies who come into school. These people will often be concerned with children who have special educational needs, for example educational psychologists or specialists from the local behaviour management unit. You may have more contact with these people if you are an individual support assistant supporting one child.

The role of the school governors

Every school has a governing body which is responsible, along with the headteacher, for making decisions about the school. It will be made up of several separate committees such as Finance Committee and Curriculum Committee which should meet regularly and report back to the main governing body. Members of a governing body will usually include parents, teachers and other members of the community who may not have direct links with the school but have an interest and may be able to offer expertise in other areas. They may or may not be regular visitors to the school but should be available when needed.

Knowledge into action

What can you find out about the role of the governors within your school? Is there a governor representative for the non-teaching staff?

The role of the Headteacher

The headteacher is responsible for managing all aspects of the school, as well as making sure that the curriculum is being effectively taught and managed. The headteacher needs not only to manage the school but maintain links with all external influences such as the local education authority. It is important that the headteacher is a member of all the committees on the school's governing body and attends all meetings.

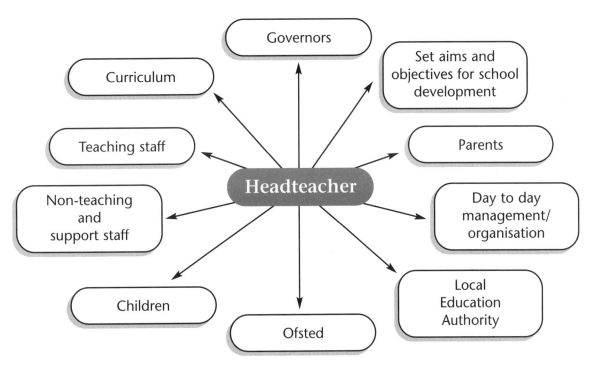

▲ The role of the headteacher is to manage all aspects of the school

The role of the deputy

The deputy headteacher's role is to work with the headteacher to manage the school. The deputy may or may not have a teaching role and will need to liase with the headteacher on a daily basis about what is happening that day. Other duties will include areas such as arranging for supply cover when staff are absent. If the headteacher is absent from the school for any reason, the deputy will take over responsibility for managing the school.

Year group, Key Stage or subject managers

Year group, Key Stage or subject managers will have responsibility for managing a group of teachers within their year or key stage or for managing a subject across the school. They may be members of the school's senior management team (SMT) and along with the headteacher and deputy will be involved with decisions about practical and day-to-day issues in the school.

These may be:

▷ arranging the school calendar (dates for the year)

▷ planning extra-curricular activities (such as sports days)

▷ discussing areas for development in the school (School Improvement or Development Plan)

▷ organisation of staffing.

Members of the SMT should meet on a regular basis and then pass information to their own teams later through year group or at subject leaders' meetings. They may also need to discuss issues within their own teams and then report back to the SMT.

Think about it

Who is your manager within the school? Are they a member of the senior management team? How often do you meet with them to discuss school issues?

Special Educational Needs Co-ordinator (SENCo)

The SENCo has the responsibility of managing the children who have special educational needs throughout the school. In some schools, SENCo's may also be a member of the Senior Management Team but this will vary between schools. They will need to keep up-to-date records on all children with special educational needs and arrange all meetings, reviews and discussions with outside agencies who need to be involved. If you are an Individual Support Assistant within a school, you may find that the SENCo is your line manager, as ISA's will support children who have special educational needs.

Knowledge into action

Find out who the SENCo is in your school and ask if you can talk to them about their role. How many children do they need to manage? Who are the people with whom they need to liase in order to carry out their role effectively?

Class teachers

The class teacher is responsible for delivering the Foundation or National Curriculum to all children within the class. (see also unit 2–3 page 54 for class teachers' responsibilities) They may also be responsible for managing a subject area within the school and will help and guide teaching assistants and other adults within their class as to their duties on a daily basis.

Voluntary helpers

Depending on how lucky you are in your school, you may have a number of different volunteer helpers who are able to offer their time and expertise to support children and teachers. They will often be parents but may also be others who have an interest in the school. In your role as a teaching assistant, you may need to set up activities for voluntary helpers and ensure that they know what they are required to do, as the class teacher may not always be able to talk to them. The kinds of activities they may help with will include:

▷ hearing children read
▷ helping with school trips and outside visits
▷ helping with activities such as cooking, sewing and art
▷ being responsible for book and video clubs
▷ managing PTA activities
▷ helping with administrative tasks
▷ helping with sports days.

Think about it

Have you had to support the work of volunteer helpers within your school? What kinds of activities have you needed to talk to them about? Were you given advice and help with this by the class teacher?

Visitors from outside agencies

You may come into contact with professionals from outside the school on a regular or occasional basis. These people will usually support children with special educational needs and may also come to do observations and advise teachers and assistants.

Case study

Mandy is an individual support assistant. She is working with Edward, who is autistic. Lately, Edward has been demonstrating some quite aggressive behaviour towards other children and the SENCo has decided to hold an emergency review to discuss what is happening. All professionals involved with Edward have been invited, including Mandy. These include the educational psychologist, advisory teacher for autism, class teacher, headteacher and speech and language therapist. All those at the review will discuss Edward's behaviour and what the school's next steps should be.

Teaching assistants

Teaching assistants may have a number of titles within a school. They may also be called classroom assistants, learning support assistants, school assistants or individual

▲ You may find that in some classes there is a classroom assistant as well as an individual support assistant for a child who has a statement

support assistants. Many of these will have the same kinds of duties to perform within a school (see also Unit 2-3 for a fuller description of your role) You will probably have several teaching assistants within your school and may work more closely with some than with others, for example if they are in the same year group.

Think about it

You are working in a busy Year 2 class one day a week (you move between classes). On this particular day you need to change the childrens' reading books which the class teacher has left out for you as soon as you arrive in the morning so that the parent helper can hear the children read until playtime. Unfortunately you are late to school as you had a puncture on the way and have not had time to change the books.

What would you do in this situation and in what order?

Knowledge into action

St Joseph's Junior School

Job Description
Teaching Assistant

Responsibilities
Responsible under the direction of the headteacher or another designated teacher to assist in the classroom.

Duties
Main duties will include:

▶ assisting in classroom organisation, preparing materials and resources where appropriate
▶ supporting and supervising activities organised by the classroom teacher
▶ supervising children usually in the presence of a teacher
▶ providing general care and welfare to children
▶ any other duties as required commensurate with the level of responsibility of the post.

Look at the job description for a teaching assistant above.

1 Are there any duties which you think are missing from this job description?

2 Do you feel that your job description matches what you are asked to do in school?

See also Unit 2-3 page 54 for the teaching assistant's role.

As well as a job description, there may also be a 'Person specification', which will set out personal qualities which may be relevant to a particular post. These may include:

▷ **Be a good communicator/enjoy working with others** It is vital that an assistant is able to share thoughts and ideas with others and is comfortable doing this. This means being open and honest with your colleagues at all times.

Case study

Marion is an experienced assistant and has been at the same school for several years. Recently the school have taken on a number of new assistants who are taking classroom assistant courses. Marion is unhappy because she feels that although she is very experienced, this does not seem as important as having a qualification.

1 What should Marion do?

2 What might happen if she remains unhappy and does not speak to anyone?

▷ **Use initiative** Assistants will need to be able to sometimes decide for themselves how to use their time if the teacher is not always available to ask. There will always be jobs which need doing in a classroom, even if this just means sharpening pencils or making sure that books are tidy and in the right place.

▷ **Respect confidentiality** It should be remembered that in a position of responsibility it is essential to maintain confidentiality. Assistants may sometimes find that they are placed in a position where they are made aware of personal details concerning a child or family. Although background and school records are available to those within the school, it is never appropriate to discuss them with outsiders.

Knowledge into action

Do you know where you fit into your workplace? What are your responsibilities? Do they match your job description?

▷ **Be sensitive to children's needs** Whether an individual or classroom assistant, it is important to be able to judge how much support to give whilst still encouraging children's independence. Children need to be sure about what they have been asked to do and may need help organising their thoughts or strategies but it is the child who must do the work and not the assistant.

▲ Teaching assistants need to have a sense of humour when working with children

▷ **Have good listening skills** A teaching assistant needs to be able to listen to others and have a sympathetic nature. This in important quality for your interactions both with children and other adults.

▷ **Be willing to undertake training for personal development** In any school there will always be occasions on which assistants are invited or required to undergo training and these opportunities should be taken wherever possible. You may also find that your role changes within the school due to movement between classes or changing year groups. You will need to be flexible and willing to adapt to different expectations (see also Unit 2-4.2).

▷ **Be firm but fair with the children** Children will always quickly realise if an adult is not able to set fair boundaries of behaviour. Adults should always make sure that when they start working with children they make these boundaries clear.

▷ **Enjoy working with children and have a sense of humour** Assistants will need to be able to see the funny side of working with children and a sense of humour is often a very useful asset!

The lines and methods of communication within the school

Lines of communication within the school should be kept open through routine procedures so that each member of staff has access to new information. This is to ensure that everyone is aware of their responsibilities and knows what is happening within the school. The way in which information is passed around may vary but it can be:

▷ **through meetings** – these may be separate for governors, senior management, teaching staff, teaching assistants, midday supervisors or year groups, depending on the kind of information which needs to be shared or distributed. They may be regular, for example every Monday or as the need arises.

▷ **through a daily book or bulletin board** – this will usually be filled in on a daily basis and will give all members of staff details of what is happening on that day.

▷ **through noticeboards or newsletters** – noticeboards may be displayed inside the school or regular newsletters sent home to both staff and parents, perhaps on a particular day of the week so that they can look out for it.

▷ **through informal discussions** – staff may discuss information informally during breaks or other times outside the classroom. This is fine but it may mean that important information does not reach all members of staff.

▷ **through parent–teacher associations** – schools will usually have PTA's which give a great deal of support to them through fundraising and other activities. Information about the PTA may be displayed on noticeboards, through regular newsletters or on the school's website if it has one.

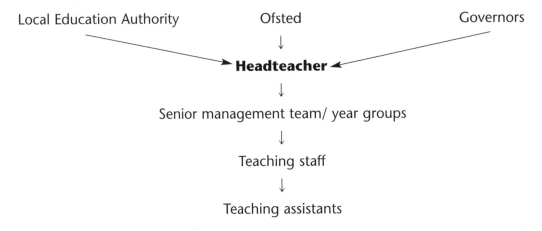

Local Education Authority   Ofsted   Governors
↓
Headteacher
↓
Senior management team/ year groups
↓
Teaching staff
↓
Teaching assistants

▲ How information moves through the school

If you are working with a class teacher, you may find that you receive information on a daily basis from them as you may have limited hours within the school and less access to general information and informal exchanges of ideas. However, as a teaching or support assistant, you should also have your own line manager or teacher who is responsible for passing on information.

If you are in a large school, there may be regular meetings especially for assistants, but if your school is smaller, it is important to make sure that you have regular access to general information.

What different systems do groups within your school have for passing on information? How do you ensure that you receive all information you are meant to?

Meetings and consultation structures

We have already seen how schools should have positive opportunities for teaching assistants to share information about the school and about pupils. It is important to make these times available as many teaching assistants work part time or work in one class with one pupil. Assistants need to have opportunities to share ideas and experiences with others so that they do not feel isolated. These should include:

▷ regular meetings for teaching assistants
▷ assistants working together to support classes or individuals
▷ assistants talking to adults from outside agencies
▷ notice-boards and year group meetings.

These meetings and opportunities for discussion do not need to be long, but are an important part of an assistant's role. They are part of a communication process which should take place within the school for passing information between all staff.

Meeting with the class teacher

When meeting with the teacher, the main areas for discussion should be the planning and evaluation of learning activities. Your class teacher may or may not be your mentor, as you may be split between classes. If your class teacher is also your mentor, you will also be discussing how your course requirements fit in to your work in school.

Your role and the role of the teacher should be one of a partnership, where there are clear roles and responsibilities for working together to support the pupils. (see Unit 2.3 on page 54) You may also be involved in planning a series of activities to be carried out over several sessions. This could be with the same group, if the children need to work on a particular idea or with different children on a similar, perhaps differentiated, task.

Ideally, assistants should be given this opportunity to input some of their own ideas into class activities when they are at the planning stage. This is because they may have their own areas of expertise or ideas that may help the teacher to formulate activities for children. This is especially true for assistants who support individual children with special needs as there will be some activities in which these children need more structured tasks.

Case study

You are working with a class as an individual support assistant for Jake who has specific learning difficulties and are meeting with the class teacher to discuss planning. When discussing the work you are going to do in numeracy, you notice that one of the concepts is going to be particularly difficult for Jake and he may need to have it simplified further.

Would you say anything to the class teacher and if so, how could you make suggestions tactfully?

You should also be aware of your own areas of weakness. For example, if you know that you will find it difficult to take a group of children for an art activity on printing because you have not done this for a long time, then say so. You should feel comfortable with what you are doing because it is important to be confident when carrying out the activity. If you anticipate any other difficulties in carrying out the plan which the teacher has not foreseen, you should also point these out.

▲ You will need to be able to point out problems which the teacher may not have foreseen

Principles underlying effective communication skills and how these may be applied within the school environment

Working as part of a team

As you will be working as part of a team you will need to have good communication, collaborative and interpersonal skills. This means that you will need to be able to get on with other members of staff and support others. These could be members of the team that you work with all the time or those who you only meet occasionally. You will need to know the principles underlying these skills so that you are able to apply them.

Principles of effective teamwork

Effective collaborative skills – this means that you will need to be able to work effectively with others for the benefit of the whole school. The kinds of skills your team should have may include:

▷ being clear about objectives and goals – understanding and knowing how the school is developing

▷ being open about confronting and resolving any problems

▷ working in a positive atmosphere of mutual support and trust

▷ conducting regular reviews with other staff

▷ having sound decision-making procedures which involve including all members.

? Think about it

What kinds of decision-making do you have to make as a team member? What do you have to refer to your teacher or another member of the school team? Think about the following decisions with your school policy in mind.

▶ Sending a child home who is ill.

▶ Making a child go for 'time out'.

▶ Sending a child to the headteacher for recognition when they have worked hard.

▶ Phoning a parent about an incident which has happened in school.

You may be in a school where you are aware of your team's objectives and goals, but you may find that you are not clear about what you are working towards as a staff member. If you find that this is a problem, you should speak to your mentor so that you are clear about your objectives.

▲ Make sure that you are not over confident and dominate the discussion

Effective communication skills – these are vital when working with others. You will need to show that you:

▷ listen to what others have to say. Always actively listen to others, so that you are aware of what they are saying to you! Make sure that you are taking in what they are saying. (see Unit 2 page 35, 'Communicate effectively with children.')

▷ make time to talk to others within your team – take up all opportunities to attend meetings so that you are aware of all that is happening within your school.

▷ are aware of your own contributions to team discussions – make sure that you contribute, even if you do not feel confident about putting your ideas across. You should also make sure that you are not over-confident and dominate the discussion.

Effective interpersonal skills – this means that you will need to be able to get along with different personalities within your work team. You may find this harder to do with some people than with others, but you should be able to relate to all members of your work team. You can do this by making sure that you are always friendly and have time to speak to all members of your team. (see also conflicts and poor communication page 95) You should be sympathetic to the needs of others and encourage those who are finding work challenging or difficult. This could be due to other factors outside the school setting which may be on their mind.

'I have just started work in my first school'

'I have just found out that I have to go into hospital'

'I have been working with the same child for the whole of primary school and now she has left and I am working with someone very different'

'My own child is having problems at school and I am worried about him'

'I am a single parent and have a sick child at home'

'My partner has just been made redundant'

▲ Issues outside school may make it difficult to concentrate on problems in the work environment

Maintaining good relationships with colleagues

As we have already seen, when you are working with others in a professional environment, it is important that you offer one another mutual support and encouragement. Because of the way in which schools are organised, you will not be able to work independently and should offer support to others in different ways. These should be:

▷ **Practical** – helping others out if they need help or advice with finding or using equipment and resources.

▷ **Informative** – helping those who do not have the right information.

▷ **Professional** – you could be in a position to help others on a professional level with issues such as planning how to carry out activities with children. You may also be asked to write records or reports on particular children.

▷ **Emotional** – it is important to support others through day-to-day events and to retain a sense of humour!

All of these methods of supporting others should be carried out consistently and effectively within the school. This means that you should always try to think of ways of helping and supporting others and take time to notice if all does not seem well.

Your school should have procedures in place to ensure that good working relationships are encouraged and promoted between colleagues.

? Think about it

Think about the different groups of people with whom you come into contact within the learning environment. This could be within the school but could also be outside, for example if you work with a child who has special educational needs and have contact with outside agencies. Do you think that you consider the following 4 methods of support when working with them?

▶ Practical

▶ Informative

▶ Professional

▶ Emotional

The difference between professional and personal relationships

When working with others as part of a team, you should be aware of the difference between personal and professional relationships. Although people often become friends through working together, it is important to establish good working relationships first. You should ensure that you consider the keys to good practice shown below. Apart from areas already discussed, such as ways in which you can support others, you will need to be able to develop other strategies for your contribution to the team. (see element 2 of this unit.)

Keys to good practice
Working with others

✔ Ensure you are considerate towards other members of your team.

✔ Carry out your duties well and cheerfully.

✔ Speak to the appropriate team member if you have a problem which you are unable to resolve.

✔ Acknowledge the support and ideas of other team members.

✔ Do not gossip or talk about other people within your team.

✔ Always be open and honest with your colleagues.

School policies for dealing with difficulties in working relationships and practices

Conflicts and poor communication within teams

You may find that sometimes areas of conflict will arise within your work team. This could be simply caused by clashes of personality, but there could also be other reasons such as conflicting ideas or poor communication between members of the team. These may be:

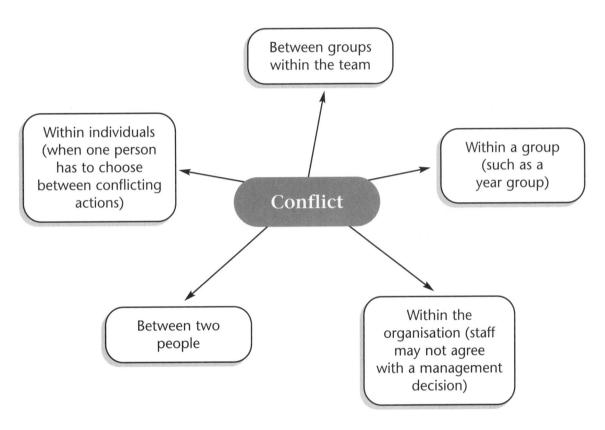

▲ Conflicts can arise within your work team

In all these cases, it is important to try to be able to discuss problems with others so that the situation does not escalate. The school may have policies and procedures for dealing with difficulties in working relationships. This will include areas such as confidentiality and you will need to know whom you should speak to and discuss any problems.

You may be able to constructively resolve issues within your team or group without involving other members of staff. You can do this by being open with others and allowing opportunities for discussion. This can sometimes be the best way of dealing with problems, although you will need to make sure that more senior members of staff do not need to be aware of them.

Case study

Debbie is a teaching assistant in Year 5. She has been working with the same teacher for 2 years. She finds out that another assistant within the junior school is to go on 2 weeks' holiday during term time and that she will have to cover her class for some of the time. Debbie is unhappy for several reasons: because she heard about this through a conversation in the staff room, she will have to work with a different teacher and she is unhappy that her colleague is able to take such a long holiday in term time.

▶ Do you think that Debbie is justified in being unhappy about this situation?

▶ Discuss what you think she should do.

Think about it

You are working between 3 Year 2 classes as a teaching assistant. Although you are happy to move between classes, on one particular week you have been asked by one teacher to put up a large display, whilst in another class you are working on literacy and you have also been asked to go on a school trip. This means you are working more hours than usual.

▶ Do you think you would have any problems with this?

▶ Would you say anything to anyone?

Evidence collection

In your evidence collection for this element, you may need to use simulation in order to obtain evidence in relation to responding to conflict situations and poor communication. Write about the following scenario.

You are going to work together with the class teacher the following week on some music activities on composing. As music is one of your strengths, you have lots of ideas for starting points to enthuse the class and would like to use your own skills on the piano. However, the class teacher has thoughts of her own and does not seem receptive to your ideas. Think about:

▶ what you could try to do to win the class teacher round.

▶ if there is anything you could do if she continued to be unreceptive?

▶ how you could use your skills in any other way or make any further suggestions?

▶ whether you need to discuss this with anyone else? Who could this be if the class teacher was also your mentor?

Element 2-4.2 Develop your effectiveness in a support role

For this element, you will need to know and understand the following:

▶ school expectations and requirements about your role, including appraisal systems

▶ how to access development opportunities.

School expectations and requirements about your role, including appraisal systems

As an assistant, you will need to make sure that you keep up-to-date with developments within your role and the kinds of responsibilities you are required to undertake. You can do this by making sure that you have regular reviews within your school that look at your job description and make sure that it is a realistic reflection of the kinds of duties you are undertaking. You should also try to find out from others whether your performance is meeting the requirements of your role.

As part of your role as a teaching assistant within a school, as with most other professions, you will also be required to think about how you can extend your own professional development. This means that you will need to think about how you are going to progress within your own career. It will usually take place once a year and is known as performance management or **appraisal**.

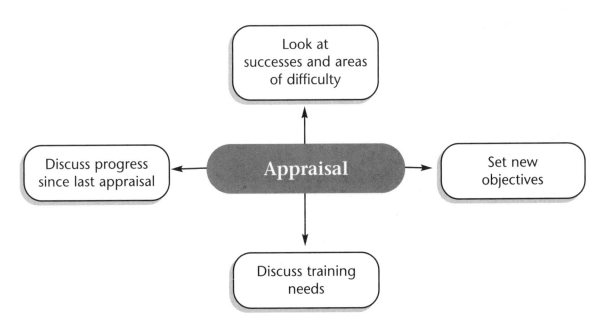

▲ What happens during an appraisal

The main consideration of appraisal is to improve staff performance, but an important part of the process is that it is positive and non-threatening. Every member of staff, including headteachers, will be appraised once a year by the person who has responsibility of managing them. In the case of the headteacher, this will usually be done by the school governors. As a teaching assistant, you will be appraised by your line manager or member of staff responsible for teaching assistants. If you are working as an individual support assistant, you may be appraised by the school's special educational needs co-ordinator (SENCo).

You may find that the appraisal process is a good opportunity to discuss any issues which may not otherwise come to light. It is also a useful time to discuss with your line manager anything which has been more or less successful than you had thought.

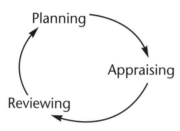

▲ The planning cycle

Before you go for your appraisal, you may be asked to fill in a general form, such as the one shown overleaf, which will help you to think about your own performance. It will also give you some idea of how your discussion might be structured.

During the appraisal, you set yourself targets for the coming year. It is important that you take an active part in setting these targets. These targets are also known as **personal development objectives.** Over the year you will work on these objectives and look at them again at the end of the year. Your targets will need to be **SMART**, that is:

▷ **Specific** – the target must say exactly what is required, for example to develop strategies for teaching numeracy skills.

▷ **Measurable** – you need to be able to measure whether the target has been achieved.

▷ **Achievable** – the target must not be inaccessible or too difficult.

▷ **Realistic** – you should ensure that you have access to any training or courses which are required.

▷ **Time-bound** – there should be a time limit to the time you have to achieve your target, for example to undertake basic computer training during the year

Think about it

To help you to think about your own appraisal, try completing some of the questions on the appraisal form shown below.

General Self-Appraisal

It would be useful if you could bring this information with you to your initial meeting, to help you to identify your needs as part of the appraisal process.

1 Do you feel that your job description is still appropriate? Do you feel that there are any changes which need to be made?

2 What targets were set at the last appraisal/when you started your job? Have you achieved your targets?

3 What are the reasons for not having achieved your targets?

4 What aspect of your job has not been as successful as you had anticipated?

5 What part of your job satisfies you the most?

6 Are there any areas of your work that you would like to improve?

7 What training have you received? Has it been successful?

8 What are your current training needs?

9 What are your needs for career development?

▲ Example of the first page of an appraisal form

If you are unable to achieve your targets for any reason, this should be recorded at the next appraisal along with the cause. You can then discuss whether to include the target next time if possible.

 Case study

Joanna has recently had her appraisal with her line manager and found that she has not achieved one of her targets. This is because she was required to undertake some additional training for teaching the Early Literacy Strategy but was unable to do it due to ill health.

1 What do you think should happen?

2 How could Joanna ensure that she is able to achieve her target at a later date?

Keys to good practice
Thinking about your appraisal

✔ Check through your job description before the meeting.

✔ Think about your strengths and successes.

✔ Think about any areas you may wish to develop.

✔ Think about any training you would like to undertake.

How to access development opportunities

Your school and college should offer you development opportunities and give you an idea about training and courses which will benefit both you and the children whom you are supporting. You may need some help with finding development opportunities if you are new to the school or unsure of how to go about it. You may be offered training and support in a variety of different ways:

▷ **through whole school based training** – this means that the school may run specific courses such as training for dyslexia, which assistants should be invited to attend on INSET days or during staff meetings. Guest speakers may be invited to the school or experienced members of staff may run them.

▷ **through a mentor or member of staff who will offer you guidance and support**

▷ **through college based training** – you may find that as part of your NVQ you are offered opportunities to develop other areas which may be important for your own development – for example computer training.

▷ **through borough networks** – your local borough or education development centre will offer courses which you may be entitled to attend. Your school's line manager will be able to advise you on how to book courses which may be relevant to your own development. Your school may also belong to a group of schools who access training needs together.

▷ **through specific courses run by your borough's special educational needs team, behaviour unit or other local organisations.** These will usually be advertised or sent to the school and displayed on noticeboards or brought to your attention at meetings.

Find out about...

Recent opportunities or INSET training which your school has offered to staff over the past year. How many of these courses have been available to teaching assistants?

If your school does not provide opportunities for development and courses, you should check with your local education authority about training for teaching assistants.

Think about it

You are working in a junior school which has 8 teaching assistants, one in each class, and have been there for 2 terms. You are required to plan and work closely with the class teacher and there is time set aside during the week to do this. However you have not been offered any opportunities for professional development or appraisal as yet.

▶ Do you think that training issues should have been discussed with you?

▶ What would you do if you were in this situation?

Evidence collection

Think about and report on how your last appraisal went **OR** look at your job description and how it relates to what you actually do within the school.

End of unit test

1 Who might be in the senior management team of a school?

2 What year groups does Key stage 2 cover?

3 Where do the school recruit members of the governing body?

4 What does the headteacher of a school do?

5 What are 3 of the different ways in which information might be passed through a school?

6 What opportunities might assistants have for exchanging information?

7 What are the 3 principles of effective teamwork?

8 Where might areas of conflict exist within a school?

9 Name the 4 ways that you could ensure that effective relationships between colleagues are maintained.

10 What are the main principles of the appraisal process?

11 How can you ensure that you make full use of professional development opportunities?

References

Adair, J., *Effective Teambuilding* (Pan, 1987)

DFES, *Performance Management in schools* (model policy)

Kindler, H.S., *Managing Disagreement Constructively* (Crisp publications, 1996)

National Occupational Standards L2 (CSC Consortium)

Woodcock, M., *Team Development Manual* (Gower publishing, 1989)

Websites

www.ofsted.gov.uk

www.teachernet.gov.uk/teachingassistants

www.tasonlinemagazine.org

Optional units

Unit 2-5 Support literacy and numeracy activities in the classroom

There are two elements to this unit. These are:

2-5.1 Help pupils with activities which develop literacy skills

2-5.2 Help pupils with activities which develop numeracy skills

This unit will help you to understand the kinds of activities you may be asked to undertake during literacy and numeracy sessions within the classroom. You will need to ensure that you are clear about the organisation of learning activities and your role in supporting groups and independent learners, as well as what children are expected to learn. You will also need to discuss with the teacher how various activities went and how the pupils responded to them.

When working with children who have special needs or who speak English as a second language, you will need to be aware of further strategies that you can use to promote their language skills. This will help them not only in literacy and numeracy but also in other subject areas across the curriculum.

Element 2-5.1 Help pupils with activities which develop literacy skills

For this element, you will need to know and understand the following:

▶ school policy for English/Welsh and how this relates to national curriculum policies

▶ how pupils develop speaking, listening, reading and writing skills

▶ how to support children and encourage them to use the full range of literacy skills

▶ working with children who have special educational needs or with children who speak English as an additional language.

School policy for English/Welsh and how this relates to national curriculum policies

As with other subjects, your school should have a curriculum policy for English or Welsh which will show how it fits in with local and national requirements for the teaching of English. This will cover pupils' reading, writing and speaking and listening skills. The National Literacy Strategy, although a non-statutory document, is now taught in many primary schools. The Foundation Stage will follow the framework of the Literacy Strategy, although pupils will not have a Literacy Hour until towards the end of the Reception year, and will follow the Early Learning Goals.

Whatever your school's policy for English, it should be broken down into three areas:

Speaking and listening: This includes any opportunities given to children for speaking and listening within the learning environment. You may be asked to assess how well children speak for different purposes or how well they listen to others.

Reading: This will include any reading which takes place in school, whether it is done individually or in groups.

Writing: This will include writing done for different purposes, such as stories or non-fiction writing and includes work done on the computer.

The National Literacy Strategy

You will need to be familiar with the structure and framework of the Literacy Strategy if you are working in a school in which it is being delivered. If your school is not following the strategy it will still be useful for you to have an idea of its structure for your own professional development. Some schools will also decide to use particular parts of the strategy which they find useful.

The purpose of the Literacy Hour is to give a structure to the way in which pupils are taught in primary schools. The Literacy Strategy then gives details of what should be taught during that time. It is useful to obtain a copy of the strategy so that you can see how learning objectives are covered and how these build on each other as the strategy progresses from Reception to Year 6. It also contains a useful glossary which may help with some of the school 'jargon' you may encounter!

The Literacy Hour is broken down as follows:

1 Whole class (15 minutes) Key Stages 1 and 2 – this should be shared text work using a big book or equivalent and should be a mixture of reading and writing as a class.

2 Whole class (15 minutes)
   Key stage 1 – this session should be focused word work, which concentrates on one part of the Literacy framework to be covered during the term, for example looking at using 'wh' words.
   Key Stage 2 – this should be a balance of word work and sentence work over the term.

3 Group/independent work (20 minutes). Key Stages 1 and 2 – children should be working independently on reading, writing or word/sentence work. The teacher should be working with one or two groups each day on guided text work, which can be reading or writing. Assistants may also be working with a group to support the day's learning objectives.

4 Whole class (10 minutes) – this plenary session gives the class a chance to review and think about what they have learned during the session. It is also a good opportunity to show others what they have done.

(for a more detailed definition of these, see pages 11–13 of the National Literacy Strategy)

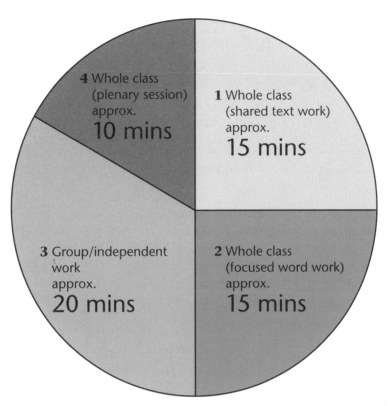

▲ Structure of the Literacy Hour

 Knowledge into action

As a group, look at the National Literacy Strategy framework for teaching. Find your own Year group's current termly plan within the strategy. Can you find specific learning objectives that you have worked on with children?

How pupils develop speaking, listening, reading and writing skills

As you will be supporting pupils during literacy sessions, you will need to understand how they develop their speaking, listening, reading and writing skills within the classroom and the opportunities that they have for doing this.

When pupils are developing their language skills, they are learning to communicate with others. The three areas of language interact with each other to promote the child's self expression and imaginative skills. Through the curriculum, pupils explore the way in which language works so that they are able to use this knowledge in a variety of situations.

Think about it

Jamie is working with a group of Year 3 children who are discussing their favourite hobbies and pastimes. She is encouraging all members of the group to contribute to the discussion and is questioning the children so that they can lead the conversation.

Sam is working in a Year 1 class that is being visited by a Road Safety Officer. The children have to sit quietly for some of the demonstration and are then invited to come forward and help and also to ask questions.

How are these 2 situations using different speaking and listening skills?
What skills will be the same?

Speaking and listening skills

Children will need to have skills in speaking and listening not only to help them to develop their reading and writing skills, but their skills across the whole curriculum. This is because children will need to be able to describe and discuss work that they are doing.

How these skills develop: According to the Foundation Stage curriculum for Communication, Language and Literacy, children will develop skills in speaking and listening through being given a variety of situations in which they can:

▷ use language to imagine and recreate roles and experiences

▷ interact with others both in play situations and to accomplish tasks

▷ demonstrate attentive listening and responses.

Think about it

Ask if you can observe children in a Reception class or local Nursery. What opportunities are they being given to use language in these kinds of situations? How can staff ensure that these kinds of opportunities are being given on a regular basis?

The National Curriculum sets out the skills which are to be developed in Key Stages 1 and 2 through being integrated into other curriculum areas. These include:

▶ focusing on the listener

▶ organising what they say

▶ sustaining concentration while listening

▶ responding appropriately to others

▶ taking turns when speaking in a group

▶ participating in drama activities

The National Curriculum pages 44 and 50 contains a much more detailed look at requirements for speaking and listening.

How you can help children to develop speaking and listening skills: you will need to show children that you are interested in what they have to say and give them your full attention. This can sometimes be difficult in a busy classroom, and although children also need to learn to wait until it is a good moment, you should ensure that when you are interacting with them it is clear to them that you are listening. This is because if you are only half interested or doing something else when they are talking to you, they will get the message that you are not giving them your full attention and may feel that they are not worth listening to. They may also think that it is alright not to listen to adults when they are talking if nobody listens to them.

When children are speaking and listening to one another, you may find that you need to give them some encouragement! Children will always find it easier to speak than to listen and will be keen for others to hear their ideas but not so keen to listen to those of others. You can do this by gently explaining to more enthusiastic children that everyone needs to have the chance to say what they think. In classes where there may be a 'showing' time or given opportunities for children to talk, it may be best to say that it is a particular group's turn on each day of the week so that they all know when they will have a chance to say something. You may also need to prompt them to respond to what others are saying, therefore checking that they are listening. Similarly when children need to sit quietly and listen during times such as assembly or if there is a visiting speaker, they should know what is expected of them.

Keys to good practice
Developing speaking and listening skills

✔ Give children eye contact when they are talking to you.

✔ Smile and give children encouragement when they are talking. You may need to make sure that shy or reticent pupils are involved in speaking and listening activiites.

✔ Repeat back what children have said to you, for example, 'Yes, you are right, Alex has worked very hard on that model'.

✔ Ask children open-ended questions so that they are encouraged to answer in more detail, rather than with 'Yes' or 'No' answers.

✔ Model the correct use of language, especially if children misuse or make up words, by repeating back the sentence correctly.

✔ Ensure that children understand what they have been asked to do by the teacher and remind them about teaching points.

✔ Encourage children to listen to each other – prevent them from interrupting and prompt them to respond to each other.

Speech bubbles: "I bringed my own lunch today instead of school dinners" "You brought your own lunch? That sounds good."

▲ You may need to model language by repeating back its correct use for children

Case study

Ralf and Nicola are using measuring equipment to find out the length of some different areas in the school. You are working with them and have been asked to make sure that they discuss what they have found out using appropriate language. In groups, think of the kinds of questions you could ask the children to make sure that they understand:

1 what they have been asked to do

2 what they have found out.

You may like to do this activity as a role-play exercise.

How pupils develop reading skills

You will need to have some idea of the basic principles by which children learn to read so that you are able to support its development. Children use a range of different strategies when learning to read so that they are able to make sense of what they are reading. These include:

▷ **Phonic cues:** children look at the sounds which make up words and this enables them to 'sound out' what the word might say. For example, a simple 3 letter word such as 'man' is sounded out easily using children's knowledge of sounds, once they have learned how to link the sounds together.

▷ **Contextual cues:** this means that children will look at the setting of the text and the kinds of words which may come up as a result. For example, if they know that the book is about the weather, they may be able to work out an unfamiliar word.

▷ **Picture cues:** children will look at illustrations in books, particularly in the very early stages of reading, as these will help them to get a 'feel' of what the book is about. It is very important for this reason not to cover up the pictures!

▷ **Grammatical cues:** children will be able to make sense of the structure of sentences through their knowledge of grammar. For example, if you read a sentence to them but miss out a word, they will know what kind of word it is meant to be – a verb, an adjective and so on.

All of these cues will help the child to decipher the text through forming a system which will help them to decode its meaning. As children learn to read, they will be constantly reviewing the skills which they have already developed. The skill of reading is therefore one of constantly revising and building up a bank of sounds and then words, so that the child will be able to gradually build on previous knowledge.

Children who are more fluent readers will often be asked to find information in a text, for example during comprehension exercises. This will ensure that they have understood the key ideas within a text, whether it is fiction or non-fiction.

You should also be aware of the different stages to expect from different ages of children in school. Remember the table below shows an average and that some children will develop these skills more quickly or slowly than others.

Age	Stage of development
1–2 years	Children will enjoy looking at simple picture books. They will like identifying recognisable items in the pictures.
3–4 years	Children will be able to listen to stories and will enjoy having the same stories repeated to them. They will have favourite books and may start to 'read' books independently.
5–7 years	Children will start to recognise more words and will start to be able to read simple sentences and books. They will enjoy books for a range of purposes, for example non-fiction and poetry as well as stories.
7–11 years	Children of this age will still enjoy a variety of texts and also listen to stories being read to them. They will develop their reading skills by extending their vocabulary and understanding.

Help pupils to develop reading skills

You can help pupils to develop their reading skills when hearing them read by using different strategies to help them to make sense of the text. These may be using picture cues – looking at the picture to find any clues that might tell them what the word says. The child could also use the initial sound of the word and have a sensible guess (phonic cues). Finally they should think about what they have read in the text so far (contextual cues) and use a word which makes sense in context. This may not be the correct word, but if it makes sense the child should be praised for the attempt. If children are able readers, you should not correct any mistakes too quickly but give them the chance to self-correct. They should always be encouraged to question the sense of their reading, to re-read and to self correct. Sometimes it helps if they re-read the beginning of the sentence, leave out the unknown word, read on to the end of the sentence and then guess what the word might be.

Knowledge into action

Ask your class teacher if you can hear 2 children of different abilities read to you. Think about and use the different strategies you use to support them while they are reading. Discuss in your groups what you have found out.

Keys to good practice
Developing reading skills when hearing children read

✔ Make sure the child is holding the book and turns the pages themselves – this gives them 'ownership' of the reading.

✔ Encourage the child to discuss the cover, illustrations and different scenarios or ideas in the text.

✔ Ask children questions about key points in the text.

✔ Try to encourage the child to point to each word as they are developing early reading skills.

✔ Encourage children to self-correct and make sure what they have said makes sense.

✔ When possible, ask children to tell you what might happen next or how a story might end. Alternatively ask them if they can tell you what has happened so far. This ensures that they understand what they are reading.

Factors that will hinder children's learning when learning to read include:

▷ not enough time to hear individual children read

▷ unsuitable learning environment, for example conditions which make it difficult for pupils to concentrate such as excess noise or other discomforts

▷ having a book which is not the right 'level' for the child. If this happens to you, you will need to speak to the teacher before continuing.

How pupils develop writing skills

The skills of reading and writing are very closely interlinked: the two reinforce each other. Children will develop writing skills through being given opportunities to use their knowledge of phonics for a variety of different purposes. At the earliest stages of writing, support for pupils will focus on correct pencil grip and letter formation, which may or may not be cursive (joined), although joined writing should be encouraged by Year 2. You should encourage pupils to follow the correct letter formation so that they start to write more fluently. Children may be provided with a pencil grip or wider pencil if they are finding it difficult to hold the pencil correctly. As children become more confident and learn their letters and sounds, they will start to use phonics to help them break down words and eventually to write independently.

At the earliest stages of writing, children will need to have support to show them how to word build and to keep them focused on their writing. As they become more confident and able writers, they will be able to concentrate more on the development of ideas. Through different ways of writing, they will learn how to put these ideas into words and sentences. They may need to be given varying degrees of support when they reach this stage, to help them to structure and organise their written work.

▲ The correct pencil grip is important when learning to write

▲ Correct letter formation is important from an early stage

Children should also have opportunities to write for different reasons, for example:

▷ making lists and writing instructions

▷ writing a variety of stories and rhymes

▷ writing letters

▷ writing dialogue

▷ presenting the case for an argument

See the Literacy Strategy framework for a comprehensive list of what children need to learn.

Help pupils to develop writing skills

In order to help pupils to develop writing skills, you will need to encourage and support what they are doing. It is useful to have some idea of the level of the children with whom you are working, as sometimes children will say that they 'can't do it' in order to have support without trying! However, it will be difficult for them to make progress if they are always reliant on others. You will need to be able to encourage children to have a go at saying what they want to, without fear of criticism. If you need to point something out which is incorrect, you should always balance it with something positive. For example, it would be better to say, 'Well done, you have had some really good ideas with your description of the Iron Man. Are there any other describing words you can think of?' than 'You haven't really given me much idea about what the Iron Man is like with your description.'

Age	Stages of writing development
3–4 years	Children will start to have more control over their fine motor skills. They will be able to control a pencil or crayon and make deliberate strokes on a page.
4–5 years	Children may be able to write their name and will start to write some letters and words, although these may not be correctly formed or oriented. They will start to learn that letters relate to spoken sounds. Progress may still be limited to the mechanics of writing.
5–6 years	Children will make progress in writing and start to put more words together. At this stage, progress may be quite different between children.
6–7 years	Children will begin to focus on the context and setting of their writing. They will start to be more aware of points such as grammar and spelling strategies and begin to use dictionaries.
7–9 years	As children become more experienced writers, they will need to take into account audience, text structure, and effective use of vocabulary.
9–11 years	Children should have learned how to look constructively at their own or others' work and be able to check and redraft.

Knowledge into action

Ask your mentor if you can observe writing sessions in different classes and age groups. Look at the different ways in which teachers and assistants support children with their writing and how children are asked to write for different purposes.

Keys to good practice
Developing writing skills

✔ Ensure children are holding the pencil and forming letters correctly.

✔ Help children to structure what they want to say.

✔ Ask children to read back and check through what they have written.

✔ Make sure that any word banks, lists or dictionaries are available for use.

✔ Ensure children have opportunities to write for a variety of purposes.

✔ Encourage children to make an attempt writing on their own first.

Additional strategies for supporting children during literacy sessions

At the time of writing, the government have introduced 3 literacy support programmes designed to focus on children who are not making the same progress as their peers but who may do with some additional help. These are:

▷ **Early Literacy Support (ELS) (Year 1)**
▷ **Additional Literacy Support (ALS) (Year 3)**
▷ **Further Literacy Support (FLS) (Year 5)**

These 3 strategies have all been introduced into schools at different times since September 2001 and are run mainly by teaching assistants. They provide learning materials and lesson plans for a set number of sessions to help children to 'catch up'. Children are encouraged to identify their learning targets and to assess their own progress. Assistants will need additional training in order to deliver these programmes effectively, as well as being thoroughly familiar with the Literacy Strategy for that year group. The 3 programmes are not statutory but it is hoped that schools will take advantage of the additional learning materials.

 Find out about...

If any of these programmes are being used in your school and whether they are run by assistants. How many children are being targeted in each of the 3 year groups?

Working with children who have special educational needs or who speak English as an additional language

These two areas may both be managed in a school by the SENCo, but you should remember that children who speak English or Welsh as an additional language will not necessarily have special educational needs. This is because most children in the school environment will pick up a second language relatively quickly. However, some of the strategies which you use to support children with particular special educational needs may also be applicable to those who speak English as an additional language.

Children who have special educational needs

Children in your school may have a wide range of special educational needs. You may be working with one of these children as an individual support assistant and need to be with them every day or you may work as a teaching assistant in a class which has children who have special educational needs. You will need to ensure that you understand what the child's needs are and the areas on which they need to work. The kinds of special educational needs children may have are shown in the table below.

Different kinds of special educational needs
Communication and interaction needs such as speech and language delay or disorders.
Cognition and learning needs which can be moderate, severe or profound.
Behavioural, emotional and social development needs which will have an effect on how the child interacts with others.
Sensory or physical impairment – this will affect the child's senses.

Children with some special educational needs will need to have additional help in order to access learning activities in a mainstream school. As an assistant, you will need to be able to help them to do this across the curriculum. You should always agree with the class teacher the strategies to be used with children who need extra help or who have specific educational targets. There may also be input from agencies outside school which will support the staff and help to set targets for the child. These may be addressed in the child's Individual Education Plan (IEP), which sets out these targets on a regular basis (see also page 34 for an example of an IEP).

Specialist support from outside agencies

▶ **Speech and Language Unit** – will give support to children with a range of difficulties, from minor speech impairment to more complex language disorders.

▶ **Sensory Support Service** – deals with difficulties such as permanent sensory or physical impairment, including deafness and blindness.

▶ **Complex Communications Service** – will diagnose and advise on disorders such as those in the autistic spectrum.

Supporting children with communication and interaction needs

These children may need support to enable them to communicate with others, so a difficulty in this area will particularly affect a child's speaking and listening skills. This may vary from a speech impediment to more complex speech and language disorders and will also include conditions such as autism, where children's social interaction is affected. To help children with these needs you will need to:

▷ ensure you have up-to-date information about the child's language and communication skills

▷ actively encourage the child to participate in learning activities and be aware of learning objectives and individual education plans

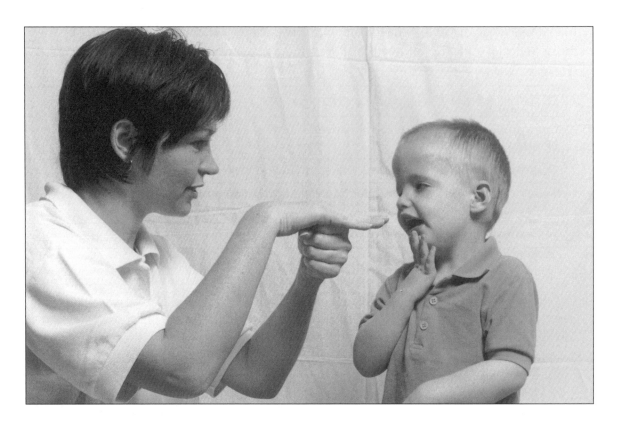

▲ Some children may need support to enable them to communicate

▷ reinforce spoken language wherever possible – this may need to be done through signing
▷ encourage the child to respond to others
▷ adapt the layout of the room where necessary.

Supporting children with cognition and learning needs

These children may have a specific learning need such as dyslexia or a more severe learning difficulty which prevents them from achieving at the same level as their peers. You will need to be able to help children to structure their learning so that they can begin to develop independence skills. You can do this by:

▷ ensuring children have set routines so that they know what to do
▷ helping children by using cues such as visual timetables so that they know what will happen each day
▷ checking that you have up-to-date information about the child's needs and what they are expected to learn
▷ liasing with the teacher and modifying work where necessary.

It is very important when working with children who have these kinds of needs that you remember only to intervene where necessary and to provide support through encouragement rather than doing it for the child. This is because children need to have opportunities to develop skills such as decision making, problem solving and exercising choice.

 Case study

Lianne has dyslexia and is in Year 2. She goes to a small group for extra literacy support and is making progress although this is slow.

Ashok is in the same class and is autistic. He has a good grasp of his sounds but is very untidy and rushes his work.

Discuss how you could help and encourage these 2 children when working individually in class.

Supporting children with behaviour, emotional and social development needs

These children will need to be supported by a whole school approach to behaviour management. (see also unit 3.1 on page 143) This means that all staff will need to be aware of children who have these needs and a consistent approach taken across the school. Your school should have a behaviour management policy which will give you the school's guidelines for the types of sanctions and strategies which should be used. In order to help these children in both literacy and numeracy you will need to promote good self-esteem through recognising their efforts and encouraging them to take responsibility for their own behaviour.

Supporting children with sensory or physical impairment

These children may be supported by a range of specialist advisory teachers, physiotherapists and other professionals who may come into school. If you are supporting a child who has a physical impairment, you will need to make sure that you are up-to-date with the nature and level of their needs. They may also need to have specialist equipment to enable them to access the curriculum.

Within literacy and numeracy tasks, these children may find it helpful to have access to a computer. You will need to:

▷ make sure you are fully aware of the child's physical and educational needs

▷ ensure you have detailed information from the class teacher about the planned learning tasks and objectives

▷ adapt the learning environment and materials where necessary to enable pupils to participate alongside their peers

▷ assist and encourage pupils and give positive reinforcement.

Children who speak English as an additional Language (EAL)

In your school, there may be children who speak English or Welsh as an additional language. The number of children will vary between schools, but you will need to be able to encourage children who speak English as an additional language to participate in learning activities to develop their literacy skills. These children will come from a variety of home and educational backgrounds and each child will have different needs. You should find that your school offers you support both through the SENCo and class teacher if you are working with an EAL child. The school may also have support through an EAL tutor who will come into schools to support and advise classroom teachers.

Strategies for classroom teaching and learning for EAL pupils

Assistants will need to work together with teachers and EAL tutors when supporting children in classrooms to enable them to develop their language skills effectively. Planning and development should be clear so that each child is encouraged to respond and to further their own knowledge of language. It is important to have specific strategies in place so that all staff have clear ideas about how these children may be supported. It is also important for staff to consider the abilities and needs of individual children and to get to know them, as they may have particular strengths in different curriculum areas.

Speaking and listening skills

This is the most important area to be developed in EAL children and you may find that you are working with individuals or small groups to do this. In very young children the approach may be different from junior school children, but the strategies should be the same and should apply across the curriculum.

▷ **Finding opportunities to talk** – children will need to be given as much opportunity as possible to talk and discuss ideas with others. At a very young age this will include opportunities such as role-play, whereas older children may enjoy discussions.

▷ **Using physical cues and gestures** – for example thumbs up, thumbs down. This will enable the child to make sense of the situation more quickly.

▷ **Songs and rhymes** – children will develop concepts of pattern and rhyme in language through learning nursery rhymes and songs. They are also an enjoyable way of developing the children's language skills as well as being part of a group. You may also be able to introduce rhymes and songs in other languages for all the children to learn and so develop their cultural awareness.

▷ **Using games** – these kinds of opportunities are useful as they will help children to socialise with others as well as practice their language skills.

▷ **Using practical examples** – these can be used to help children when they are being given instructions, for example showing a model when the children are going to do group work.

▲ Physical gestures can help when communicating with EAL children

▷ **Discussing with a partner first** – this may help EAL children to gain confidence when they have to tell their ideas to the class. They should work with a variety of children who will provide good role models.

▷ **Use vocabulary which is appropriate** – staff will need to think about the language that they use with bilingual and multilingual children to ensure that it is appropriate to the child's age and level of understanding. If the teacher is talking to the class and has used language which is difficult to understand, assistants may need to clarify what has been said for them.

▷ **Using purposeful listening** – if children have come into school with very limited experience of the target language, assistants may be asked to work with them on specific areas of language. For example, the teacher may be focusing on positional words to ensure that the child understands words such as behind, above, below, next to and so on. You may work with pictures or other resources to help the child to develop their understanding of these words.

▷ **Explain the purpose of the activity** – children should be aware of why they are undertaking a particular activity and what they are going to learn from it.

Reading and writing skills

Children who are learning to speak English or Welsh as an additional language will need to have opportunities to read and listen to books in the target language. This is so that they can associate their developing verbal and written skills with the printed page. Bilingual children will also benefit from working with the rest of the class during the

Case study

Look at these 2 examples:

Rosanna is a refugee child who has just started school in Year 5. She has had a traumatic home background and a limited experience of school.

Paul has come from France and has entered school in Year one. He has not been to school before but speaks a few words of English.

It is important to remember the different levels of help that these children may need. Discuss in your groups how you might start to help Rosanna and Paul with their language skills when they first enter school.

Literacy Hour. They will be able to share texts with the whole class and with groups of children, although teachers may need to use additional strategies so that they maximise learning opportunities. These should be clear to teaching assistants so that they can support the children through reinforcing the skills which are being taught. These kinds of strategies may include:

▷ using repetitive texts
▷ revising previous weeks' work to build confidence
▷ using pictures more in order to point out individual words
▷ pacing the lesson to enable bilingual children to have time to read the text
▷ grouping EAL children according to their actual ability rather than their understanding or knowledge of English.
▷ praising and encouraging children wherever possible
▷ using computer programs to help with reading.

You could also refer to the 'Keys to good practice when developing speaking and listening skills' on page 109.

Children who are learning to speak English or Welsh may need to decipher the meaning of some words with adult support when they are learning to read. They may need more support during Guided Reading* sessions but should benefit from these as they will be able to model good practice from other children. As with all children they will need to experience a wide variety of texts, both fiction and non-fiction, in order to maximise their vocabulary. It may be that the child is able to read and understand more than has been expected: in this case staff should always continue to extend their vocabulary by discussing the text further.

After consultation with the class teacher, assistants may find that they need to adapt and modify learning resources used with the child or children. This will help them to access the curriculum more fully. Assistants may also need to explain and reinforce vocabulary which is used in the classroom, for example during a topic. Often, the kinds of resources which benefit bilingual children will also be useful for other children in the class or group.

*Guided Reading is an activity which takes place in small ability groups (usually around 6 children), using a set of books which are the same. The books should be slightly challenging so that the children need to think about some of the words. Children will then read the books independently while the teacher or assistant supports them. During this time the children will be looking at a variety of cues to help them to decode the text. It is important that during guided reading, teachers and assistants help children by encouraging them to use all these cues together.

Problems which may occur when providing support for bilingual pupils

The kinds of problems which may occur when supporting bilingual pupils may be short term or long term. If the group or individual which is being supported for a particular activity is finding it too challenging, you may need to modify or change plans to accommodate this, as it will not always be possible to speak to the teacher immediately. However, it is important that the teacher is informed as soon as possible in order to inform future planning. Some pupils may take a long time to become confident in a second language, and it will be apparent that they understand much more than they are able to say. This is not unusual and staff will not be able to push children into talking before they are ready. The most important thing to do is to encourage and praise children wherever possible, repeating back to them so that they develop a positive view of themselves.

Where pupils have a specific learning difficulty, this can take longer to detect if they are bilingual. This is because staff may feel that they are finding school more difficult owing to their development of the target language. If you find that a particular child is not able to manage the tasks set and is not progressing, you should always speak to the class teacher.

Other problems could include inadequate or unsuitable resources, and disruptions within the learning environment as outlined in Unit 2.1.

Keys to good practice
Teaching bilingual and multilingual pupils

✔ Group with children of similar ability.

✔ Use strategies which develop self esteem and confidence.

✔ Provide visual and physical supports to help understanding.

✔ Model language using other children.

(You may also look at The Teaching Assistant's Handbook S/NVQ Level 3 for a full chapter on supporting children with special educational needs and bilingual and multilingual pupils.)

 Evidence collection

For your evidence for this unit, ask your school's SENCo if you can work with a child who has a specific language need, for example dyslexia, over a period of time. Speak to the class teacher about work which you could do to support the child and tie in with his or her learning targets. Track the child's progress through recording learning objectives and outcomes over the period and record some of your interactions with the child.

You may like to use the following format:

> **Name:** For the purpose of the evidence you will need to change the child's name
>
> **Date:**
>
> **Preparation/materials:** Make sure you are prepared and have everything that you need
>
> **Activity/learning objective:** ensure you have clear objectives
>
> **Interactions:** make notes about interactions between you and the child or the child and other children which are particularly interesting.
>
> **Analysis:** How well did the child respond? Did he or she understand? How did he or she show you that he understood? What might you do differently next time?

Element 2-5.2 Help pupils with activities which develop numeracy skills

For this element, you will need to know and understand the following:

▶ the school's policy for mathematics and how this relates to national and local frameworks and policies

▶ how pupils develop mathematical skills and how to support and maintain pupils' interest in using mathematical skills

▶ working with children who have special educational needs

The school's policy for mathematics and how this relates to national and local frameworks and policies

Your school will have a policy for mathematics which will outline how the subject is taught in school. If you are working in a school in England, your school may follow the National Numeracy Strategy, while schools in Wales will follow the National Curriculum for Wales.

You may find that the way in which mathematics is taught in schools is very different from your own experiences in the subject. This is because there is a much greater emphasis, particularly in the early primary phase, on teaching children different ways of arriving at an answer and showing them a variety of ways of working. The National Numeracy Strategy is designed to give children a firm grounding in basic skills and to encourage them to think about their answers. For example, instead of giving children pages of sums they will be taught more mental strategies first so that they will have an awareness of what kind of answer is likely.

Structure of the National Numeracy Strategy and numeracy lesson

The daily mathematics lesson will be between 45 minutes and one hour and Years 1–6 will have the same structure:

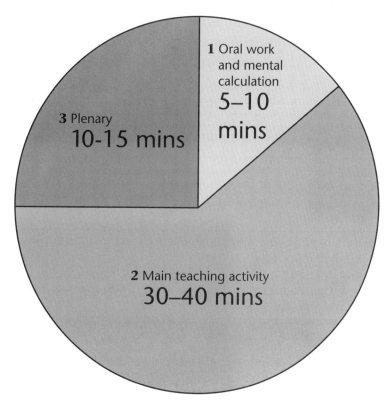

▲ Structure of the Numeracy lesson (between 45 and 60 minutes)

1 Whole class oral and mental work (5–10 minutes) to sharpen and develop children's oral and mental skills.

2 Main teaching activity (30–40 minutes), which will usually start with the whole class and then children will move into groups, pairs or individually to work on the focus of the lesson.

3 Plenary (10–15 minutes) – a whole class activity which will finish the lesson and summarise what has been learned, perhaps with examples of children's work.

Children who are in Reception will usually learn numeracy skills through part of an integrated day and work towards a more structured numeracy session towards the end of the year.

There are five strands under the numeracy framework. The first 3 (numbers and the number system, calculations and solving problems) have direct links to the National curriculum programme for the study of number. The fourth strand is linked to shape, space and measures and the fifth incorporates handling data. Using and applying maths is integrated over the five strands, that is, children need to be able to apply what they have learned through these strands into different situations. For the purpose of this element, we will look closely at the following 3 areas:

Number – using and applying number when solving problems and in practical tasks.

Shape, space and measures – this includes topics such as time, length, weight, and money.

Handling data – this includes transferring information into graphs and charts.

Children should be given the opportunity to work on all of these areas of mathematics. The key objectives for numeracy within each year group are listed within section 2 of the strategy. These objectives will build on one another throughout a child's time in school so that they develop their knowledge, understanding and skills.

You will need to have an awareness of the skills that children in your class are working towards in order to support them fully and help them to access the curriculum. The

Examples of key objectives from Reception, Year 2 and Year 6:	
Reception	Say and use the number names in order in familiar contexts. Count reliably up to 10 everyday objects. Use language such as circle or bigger to describe the shape and size of solids and flat shapes.
Year 2	Count, read, write and order whole numbers to at least 100 and know what each digit represents. Know by heart facts for the 2 and 10 multiplication tables. Use the mathematical names for common 2–D and 3–D shapes; sort shapes and describe some of their features.
Year 6	Multiply and divide decimals mentally by 10 or 100 and integers by 1000 and explain the effect. Solve simple problems relating to ratio and proportion. Read and plot co-ordinates in all 4 quadrants.
Source: National Numeracy Strategy Key Objectives	

Numeracy Strategy clearly sets these out in the teaching programmes for each year group and each term. It also gives examples of the kinds of activities which can be used with children.

Your school's mathematics policy should give a breakdown of the aims and objectives of the schools teaching of mathematics. Staff should refer to the maths policy and Numeracy Strategy, which together will give guidelines for the way in which maths is to be taught in school.

 Knowledge into action

Ask your mentor if you can look at your school's mathematics policy. Look at how it relates to the numeracy strategy and how the two relate to one another.

How pupils develop numerical skills

As with learning to read and write, pupils will develop numerical skills at a different rate depending on their understanding and existing knowledge. It is very important when introducing new ideas to children that they are given the opportunity to use practical tasks to help them to understand the principle of what they are doing. Some children will need longer than others at this stage, and they will not be able to move on until they have a clear understanding of what they have been asked to do.

How you can help children to develop their understanding and use of number

You will be asked to work with groups of children and individuals to help them to understand and use number. When working on number activities with children, you will need to work with class teachers to ensure that you understand the learning objectives of the lesson, and are clear about how activities are to be taught. You will also need to know how what you are doing fits in with the rest of the class.

Building on childrens' prior knowledge

The teacher is responsible for telling you about individual children's learning needs. You will need to have up to date information about pupils' current ability to understand and use number. This may come from the class teacher, from your own observation and knowledge of the pupil or from written records or assessments. You will need also to know if they have number targets to work on, either as a group or as part of an IEP. The kinds of strategies which you use will need to be agreed with the teacher before the start of the lesson.

The kinds of strategies assistants may need to use with pupils may range from explaining tasks and following instructions, to questioning skills or giving children extension activities if they finish their task. Some IEPs may include suggested strategies for adults to use with pupils. At the end of the lesson, you will need to give feedback to the teacher about the pupils achievements to enable them to amend and maintain records and reports.

Case study

Michael is a teaching assistant working with Year 4. He has been asked to work with a group of children who are making 'number stories' to solve simple problems. The children are having difficulty in working out how to transfer a particular problem into a number story and Michael has not had clear instructions about exactly how to help them if they have problems.

Their problem is to make up number stories to reflect the following statements:

$462 + 232 = 694$ $40 \times 3 = 120$

$88 - 24 = 64$ $36 \div 4 = 9$

For example, 3 cans of lemonade at 40p each cost 120p or £1.20 altogether.

1 What should Michael have done if he was not clear about the task?

2 How do you think he can help the children?

Helping pupils to interpret and follow instructions

Children may sometimes find that they do not understand what they have been asked to do and this may be for a variety of reasons. Some pupils may have special needs and require help to understand the task through further explanation or work more specific to these needs. Others may have not been listening to what the teacher has said or have found the explanation hard to understand. You will need to be able to explain what their instructions mean and clarify tasks, through finding out exactly how much the child did understand as a starting point.

Case study

An example of helping pupils to interpret instructions may be a Year 3 class who are starting to learn about division and how it is the reverse of multiplication. Their task is to work through a series of division questions through using multiplication strategies, for example 'Solve $28 \div 4$ by saying how many fours make 28'.

The children need first of all to think about their multiplication tables to start to solve this task. They will have to be able to put maths equipment into groups of 4 if they need practical examples to help them to visualise the problem. They may then need to write it down to see the pattern, for example:

$4 \times 7 = 28$ so $28 \div 4 = 7$

Questioning and prompting pupils

Pupils will need to be questioned when working on maths activities and assistants should know the different ways they can do this. The Numeracy strategy booklet 'Mathematical vocabulary' gives ideas for these and gives examples of different types of question:

▷ Recalling facts, for example 'What is 5 add 6?'

▷ Applying facts, for example 'Tell me how you would find out how far it was from one side of the playground to the other.'

▷ Hypothesising or predicting, for example 'Estimate how many multilink cubes will fit in the container.'

▷ Designing and comparing procedures, for example 'How could you subtract 47 from 93?'

▷ Interpreting results, for example 'What do you notice about numbers ending in 7 when you look at the number square?'

▷ Applying reasoning, for example 'How many different ways can 3 eggs go into an egg box?'

These different kinds of questions show the ways in which we can challenge children by giving them open rather than closed questions when working on maths activities. You should always try to ask the child as much as possible by guiding them round the task rather than giving them direct instructions.

 Case study

You are working with a Reception child who is doing a simple sorting activity using different coloured shapes. She has to sort a group of shapes using her own criteria and then see if there is any other way they can be sorted. What kinds of questioning could you use with the child?

Helping pupils to select and use appropriate resources

You should make sure that you are always familiar with and know the location of any resources that pupils have been asked to use. Pupils may need help with this if they have been asked to carry out an activity and are unfamiliar with mathematical resources. Children with whom you are working may not have used some items before and younger children should be given the opportunity to look at and explore them before starting to use them.

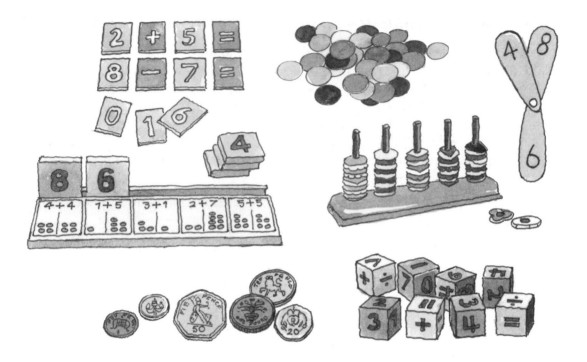

▲ There are various resources available to help with different maths activities

The following types of maths equipment may be used in schools:

Multilink/unifix – small cubes used for counting activities. They can be fixed together, multilink on all sides, unifix can only be made into towers.

Number squares – these are usually 100 squares but can also be smaller, and are used for looking at patterns within number.

Number cards – simple cards with a single number on them. These can be for recognising or for ordering numbers.

Number fans – these are used for counting and are particularly useful in oral sessions, if children are able to have one each. They are simple fans of 10.

Place value cards – these are used to demonstrate how place value works, and children put them on top of one another to form numbers. Single cards will show units below 10, an overlapping card will show the tens and a further overlapping card will show a hundred number. They are usually different colours to add clarity. For example:

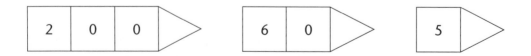

They are usually this shape so that the child knows how to place them on top of one another and can hold them without covering up the relevant numbers.

Number games – any kind of game where numbers are involved, so any game involving a dice or counting such as snakes and ladders, cards, dominoes, memory games using numbers, etc.

Dienes rods – these are also useful for place value and are plain and wooden. They come as single, small cubes which are individual units, towers of ten, squares of 100 and blocks of 100 cubes. They cannot be broken apart like unifix.

Cuisinaire rods – these are similar to dienes rods but come in different colours and each colour represents a different number. For example, one cube is pink, 2 are blue and so on, up to 10.

Number lines – these are simple lines which are used to help children when they are carrying out calculations. They may be simple at an early stage, but children who are older can devise their own to help them with calculations. For example:

A child will be able to work out 3 + 2 by starting on 3 and counting on 2 jumps. Similarly they may be used with subtraction.

As children become older and used to working with number lines, they may decide to draw lines to help them work out more complicated tasks such as 90 – 65.

If the child is able to draw a number line using tens, they will be able to see quite quickly that the answer is 25.

Scales – balance scales will often be used in infant classes, but as children become older they will use weights in them to measure things more accurately. They may also use 'proper' weighing scales but these are more easily damaged.

Rulers – will be used from around Year 2 to measure accurately.

Height charts – these will be used for measuring children's height.

Trundle wheels – these are used for measuring metres in a large area more easily than a metre stick, for example the perimeter of a playground or the length of a corridor. Each time the wheel clicks the children know they must count one metre.

Children push this handle as they walk

Clocks and timers – there will be a variety of these in schools. Clocks will usually be analogue but may also be digital, and may be real or card for children to put on their own times. Timers may be stopwatches, sand timers or balance timers which rock for only a specified time.

Reinforcing mathematical vocabulary

You may need to reinforce the use of any vocabulary which has been used by the teacher whilst explaining new concepts. This will help children to absorb new words whilst working on mathematical ideas. For example, whilst working on calculations, Year 4 pupils may be required to learn any of the following vocabulary:

Mathematical vocabulary for Year 4

Add, addition, more, plus, increase

Sum, total, altogether

Double, near double

Subtract, take away, minus, decrease

Leave, how many are left/left over?

Difference between

Is the same as, equals sign

Source: *National Numeracy Strategy, Mathematical Vocabulary* – DfES, 1999

The National Numeracy Strategy publication on Mathematical vocabulary also gives details of the kinds of vocabulary which should be used with pupils at each stage from Reception to Year 6. Assistants should be aware of the vocabulary which they can use so that they can reinforce and extend the children's learning.

Introducing follow-on tasks to reinforce and extend learning

Assistants may be asked to use follow-on tasks for those children who finish their work and have a good understanding of the concept on which they are working. These should relate to the learning activity which they have completed. For example, a Year 5 child who has just completed an exercise about odd and even numbers could be asked to carry out an investigation to find out about number patterns when using them for calculations.

Using praise to promote further learning

When you are supporting children in their mathematical development, you should always remember to use praise and encouragement as children may become quickly discouraged if they find a concept hard to understand. Children will need to experience success at their own level in order to remain motivated and on task. You will need to be able to give them constructive feedback to help them to build on what they know and encourage them in their work. This should always be appropriate to their age and area of achievement.

Case study

Look at these two comments to a Year 1 child:

A Assistant: You are doing really well with your weighing, Jack. How many different things can you find that are heavier than the multilink? When you have finished, it is Xavier's turn.

B Assistant: You need to be careful with the multilink when you are measuring, Jack, look it is going on the floor. Have you nearly finished because the others need to use some of it!

1 Why might the child be discouraged by the second comment?

2 Why should you remember to be positive about children's work?

Using calculators

Pupils should always be aware that the use of calculators is as a learning aid and not as a matter of routine. Children should be taught how to use efficient mental strategies before using the calculator. They should have their own methods for checking whether their answer is correct (see also the *Numeracy Strategy Framework* page 8 – The role of the calculator).

Keys to good practice
Developing children's use of number

✔ Be clear about learning objectives.

✔ Ensure you are up-to-date with pupils' abilities.

✔ Be aware of any individual targets such as an IEP.

✔ Use praise to support pupils' learning.

✔ Reinforce any mathematical vocabulary.

✔ Use number games to help reinforce counting skills and number recognition.

How pupils develop skills in shape, space and measures

Pupils will need to be given plenty of opportunities to explore a variety of situations with regard to shape, space and measures. They should have experiences with measuring, comparing, estimating and predicting the weight, length and volume of different materials. They should also have experiences of measuring time.

How these skills develop

The term 'shape, space and measures' applies to a range of mathematical activity in primary schools. Through this area, pupils will be learning to develop their skills in learning about shape, length, capacity and weight and time. They will also need to be able to estimate, measure and compare in these areas. Teachers and assistants will need to be able to work together to develop children's knowledge and understanding when undertaking these tasks. As with number activities, you will need to know the learning outcomes of tasks you are doing with pupils so that you can work on these together.

The National Numeracy Strategy gives the structure of how shape, space and measures are to be worked through within the Numeracy Hour. Pupils will learn how to use the vocabulary related to shape, space and measures and to use different units of measurement. It is useful to be aware of the kind of progression which is expected of pupils between Reception and Year 3, for example when thinking about measuring time as shown below:

Measuring time – a comparison from Reception to Year 6

Reception: Starting to look at the vocabulary of time through learning the days of the week and thinking about times of day such as morning, afternoon, playtime, bedtime. Children will start simple sequencing activities, through listening to stories and thinking about their own experiences. They are beginning to be aware of important times of day, for example coming to school at 9 o'clock, going to bed at 7 o'clock.

Year 1: By Year 1, pupils will be aware of different units of time and how they fit together. They will start to be able to order days of the week and the seasons. Children may also be able to read o'clock and half past on an analogue clock.

Year 2: In Year 2, pupils will start to extend their vocabulary to the names of the months and recognise when their own birthday falls. They may know other words such as fortnight, minute and second. Children will start to know that

---

▶

one week is 7 days, a day is 24 hours and so on. Children may start to estimate how long things will take, for example what might take an hour?

Year 3: By Year 3, children should be able to read the time on a digital or analogue clock to the half or quarter hour. They will continue to extend their vocabulary and estimating skills.

By **Year 6**, pupils will be using their skills at measuring time to solve problems.

Building on childrens' prior knowledge

Assistants will need to know the stage which pupils have reached in order to build on the skills they have. Children will then need to be given opportunities to use the skills which they are learning and apply them in a variety of situations. Ways in which you can find out about pupils' previous level of understanding are:

▷ **Through the teacher.** You may be informed of a child or group's understanding of a concept or stage of understanding through speaking to the teacher about work they have already completed.

▷ **Through observing the pupil.** You may know more than you think about a pupil's ability and may already be aware of the child's capabilities, through working with and watching them in class. You may also be asked to observe a child or group of children to see how they work when they are not being supported.

▷ **Through teacher or class records.** The child may already have specific learning targets or difficulties when working on shape, space and measures and you will need to be aware of these as pupils may require particular strategies to help them work on their targets.

Assistants will also need to provide feedback to the teacher after the task has been completed so that the child or childrens' records can be maintained.

Support strategies when working on shape, space and measures

Teaching assistants will need to use the same kinds of strategies when supporting children using shape, space and measures as they do with number activities. (see page 127) They should have a range of strategies which are agreed with the teacher and must ensure they have sufficient resources to carry out activities with the children. The kinds of resources which may be needed will include the following equipment:

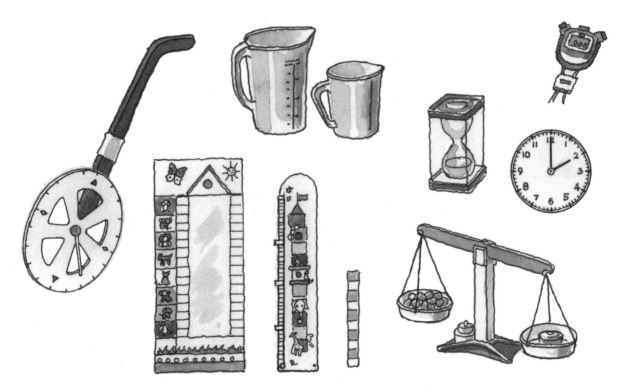

▲ A variety of measuring equipment will be needed

Resources may be kept in classrooms, or if they are to be shared between classes in a central area to which everyone has access. You will need to find out whether items need to be signed out when they are removed.

 Think about it

Think about how you might help a group of Year 2 children in the following activities:

▶ estimating and measuring the length of the corridor

▶ estimating and timing the length of time it takes to get changed for PE

▶ estimating and finding out how many unifix it will take to balance a pair of scissors.

What kinds of questioning might you use?

How could you draw on pupils' past experience to help them with the tasks?

Children will also need to learn to differentiate between different types of units of measurement and will need to have plenty of practice with each. An example of this would be 3 groups within the class working on a maths activity around the same topic, for example the topic of 'Time' in a Year 6 class.

This problem solving activity encourages children to apply what they have learned in real life situations.

▷ Lamb must be cooked for 60 minutes for every kg.

▷ Chicken must be cooked for 50 minutes for every kg.

▷ Complete this list of cooking times.

Kilograms	1	1.5	2	2.5	3	3.5
Cooking time in minutes (lamb)						
Cooking time in minutes (chicken)						
Source: National Numeracy Strategy p89, section 6						

Group 1 (highest ability) – this group might do this activity and then go on to devise their own table to use for cooking other items, or to create a graph using the table

Group 2 (middle ability) – this group might complete the activity only

Group 3 (lower ability) – this group might have a simplified version, asking them to work out only some of the table

In order to maintain pupils' interest and concentration in the task, assistants also need to remember to use encouragement and praise. These areas are interesting to children as they often include practical activities which will hold their interest. When working with younger children with equipment and practical tasks, it is worth giving them the opportunity to look at and handle shapes and equipment before starting the task. This will give them the chance to explore and become used to the equipment, so that they can focus on the activity later. However, they will still need to be kept on task and complete the learning objectives for the session.

Problems when supporting mathematical development in number and shape, space and measures.

The kinds of problems you may find when supporting children with mathematical tasks may be related to:

The child's own concept of working with mathematical tasks From an early age, teaching staff should present children with positive and fun methods of working with mathematical tasks so that they do not think of them as 'difficult' activities. Children should be given plenty of opportunities to use games, investigations and other forms of maths which develop their skills while encouraging them to be independent. Where children have trouble understanding concepts, staff must always give them opportunities to talk about their understanding and any concerns that they might have. This may be more likely to happen in a group situation rather than a

▲ Children need to be given opportunities to play mathematical games

whole class. Children can very quickly start to feel that they can't 'do' maths and lose self esteem when attempting mathematical tasks.

Case study

Hiab is in Year 4 and the class has just had a Numeracy lesson on finding the area of a circle. She is a quiet child and does not have enough confidence to put up her hand when the class teacher asks if there are any questions. You are working with her group later and notice that she is having difficulties.

1 How could you talk to Hiab without damaging her self-esteem?

2 What would you say to the class teacher?

The child's ability to learn It may be that the child is unable to complete the task because it is simply too difficult or the child has special needs which make the task very hard to complete. You may need to adapt the child's work so that they have a more realistic chance of completing it and maintaining their confidence and self-esteem.

Case study

Adrian is in Year 1 and has been diagnosed with pervasive developmental disorder, which is a mild form of autism. Although Adrian is usually able to join in with whole class activities and does not have his own support assistant, he finds some activities difficult. You are working with his group who are measuring the length of a table using their handspans. Adrian has become anxious because he can see that this will not be an accurate way of measuring the table.

1 How could you reassure Adrian if he continues to be distressed?

2 What would you do with the rest of the group if Adrian needed to be removed from the activity?

If the child has difficulties with behaviour, staying focused and being undisruptive, you may need to speak to the class teacher so that others are not disturbed. If the teacher is busy you will need to remove the child from the activity by sending them to work alone to enable you to work with the group.

The learning environment Children can be easily distracted, especially at a very young age, so they will need to have an environment which maximises the

▲ Staff must ensure that equipment is in working order before the lesson begins

opportunities for learning. The area will need to have sufficient space and be comfortable for everyone to work in. There should be a minimum amount of noise and children or support staff should not be disturbed by others when carrying out tasks.

Resources Children must have access to the resources they need when they are working. Staff must also ensure that any equipment they need to use is in working order, has batteries and so on. If items are broken or missing, this should be reported straight away so that they can be mended or replaced as soon as possible. Time can be wasted when staff have to spend lesson time sorting out these kinds of issues which should have been checked beforehand.

Additional strategies for supporting numeracy sessions

As with the literacy strategy, there are intervention programmes to help children who are slightly behind their peers to catch up with their numeracy skills. These are called 'Springboard' units and are aimed at children in each separate Year Group in junior schools. They are also designed to be used in Years 3–5 by teaching assistants supporting the teacher and are usually delivered by teachers in Year 6.

Working with children who have special educational needs

Children who have a statement of special educational needs may be working at a very different level from others in the class. You may find that you are supporting a child or children who needs specific help with mathematical tasks. The kinds of special needs which you may experience in mainstream schools may cover a wide range of difficulties, (see also page 116 for supporting SEN children during literacy activities). The child may need specific help with vocabulary or have a visual impairment which makes it difficult to use some mathematical equipment. Your class teacher will need to seek advice from the school's SENCo and other agencies outside the school for the best strategies to use with particular children. The DFES have also produced a useful publication for supporting pupils with specific needs during the daily mathematics lesson: see references on pages 141 and 142.

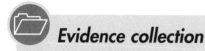

Evidence collection

Ask your mentor if you can carry out two separate maths activities with children, preferably from two different age groups. You will need to speak to the class teachers about the learning objectives of the activities and the type of support you are required to give the children. Note down what activities you carry out with the children, any learning materials they need, their responses to the activities and how you cope with any difficulties the children have in understanding what they are required to do. Make sure you give feedback to the class teacher about the pupils' progress and whether the children achieve their learning objectives and note this down in your evidence. If you are able to record the activities using a tape or a video camera this will make them particularly interesting and you may be able to watch them with others in your group.

End of unit test

1 Name the 3 areas into which English is broken down.

2 Why is the Literacy Strategy a useful tool for schools?

3 What kinds of skills will a child develop when speaking and listening?

4 How can you help pupils when developing reading skills?

5 What kinds of opportunities should pupils be given when writing?

6 What are the names of the 3 government initiatives to support literacy in schools?

7 Name 4 strategies which you could use to help children who speak English as an additional language.

8 What questioning skills might you need to use to help children with numeracy tasks?

9 How can you learn about a pupil's current level of understanding in mathematics?

10 What kinds of resources might be used to support maths?

References

Aplin, Ruth, *Assisting Numeracy: A Handbook for Classroom Assistants* (Beam)

Curriculum guidance for the Foundation Stage, DFES 2000

Fox, Glenys & Halliwell, Marian, *Supporting Literacy and Numeracy: A Handbook for Teaching Assistants* (David Fulton)

National Literacy Strategy: Framework for Teaching, DFES, 1998

National Literacy Strategy: Teachers notes modules 1–6, DFES 1998

National Literacy and Numeracy Strategies – Including all children in the literacy hour and daily mathematics lesson (DFES, 2002) Ref: DFES 0465/2002

National Numeracy Strategy – Framework for teaching Mathematics: DFES 1999

National Numeracy Strategy – Teaching mental calculation strategies at Key Stages 1 and 2 (QCA publications1999)

National Numeracy Strategy – Mathematical vocabulary: DFES 1999

Guidance to support pupils with specific needs in the daily mathematics lesson: (DFES 2001)

QCA: Planning, teaching and assessing the curriculum for pupils with learning difficulties – Mathematics (QCA/01/739)

Websites

National Autistic Society: www.nas.org.uk

http://inclusion.ngfl.gov.uk/

National Association for Special Educational Needs: www.nasen.org.uk

DfES standards website: www.standards.dfes.gov.uk/

Contribute to the management of pupil behaviour

There are two elements to this unit. These are:

3-2.1 Promote school policies with regard to pupil behaviour

3-2.2 Support the implementation of strategies to manage pupil behaviour

As a classroom assistant, you will be working alongside the classroom teacher, supporting him or her with the introduction of new activities and helping the children, either individually or in groups, to work happily and productively. Your role is very important. As we all know, groups of children, especially younger ones, can quickly get distracted and start being lively and noisy. By helping to manage the children's behaviour, through understanding their needs, anticipating any problems and smoothing them over, you will play a significant part in creating a peaceful and productive learning environment in which the children can really progress.

This section will outline your role when dealing with pupil behaviour. It will show how you need to work alongside the class teacher to support pupils and give you strategies for managing behaviour, through support which is available in school and also through other agencies. As an assistant, you should also be aware of how to promote good behaviour in schools and the ways in which you can do this.

Element 3-1.1 Promote school policies with regard to pupil behaviour

For this element, you will need to know and understand the following:

▶ the stages of social, emotional and physical development of the children you work with

▶ factors which may affect children's behaviour

▶ how to identify behaviour patterns which may indicate problems

▶ school policies for rewarding positive behaviour, managing unwanted behaviour and for children with emotional and behavioural needs

▶ how to work in line with local and national guidelines and policies.

Stages of social, emotional and physical development

Any adult who has contact with children in Early Years and Primary school settings needs to be aware of the different stages of children's development. Assistants will need to understand the way in which children learn and develop socially, emotionally and physically. In this way they will be able to support and enhance the learning process through a wider understanding of children's needs.

The stage of development in children are often divided into 4 areas:

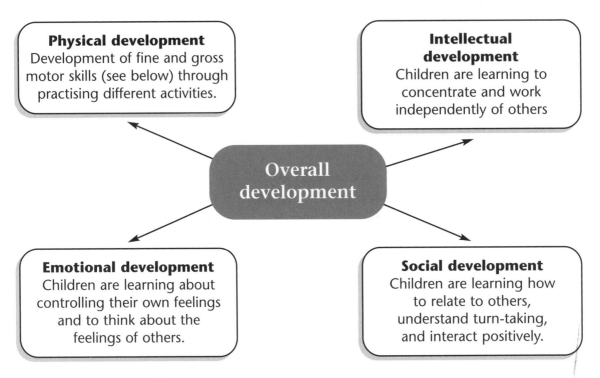

▲ The four stages of development in children

By drawing a pie chart and writing the initial letter from the 4 areas, it will give you a shortcut to remembering them (PIES). At this stage we will explore the 4 areas which affect children's behaviour (Physical, intellectual, emotional and social).

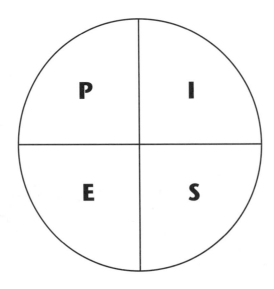

Physical development

As an assistant, you will be working with children who are developing skills through a wide range of physical activities. These may be gross motor skills, such as beginning to walk or fine motor skills, like holding a pencil. You will need to know the order in which children develop these skills, although the age at which they achieve them may differ from one child to another.

Children will undergo health checks at some of these stages to check that they are developing normally and to draw attention to any potential problems. If a child is not reaching the milestones which are expected, these can then be investigated straight away and any action taken.

▷ **Gross motor skills** – these are skills which involve large movements through the use of children's arms and legs and may include running, hopping, skipping and starting to use large apparatus such as climbing frames and other playground equipment.

▷ **Fine motor skills** – these are manipulative skills which involve finer hand control. They are vital for activities such as writing a child's own name, starting to draw recognisable pictures and colouring them in, cutting with scissors and completing jigsaws. These finer skills are vital for being able to learn to write.

▲ Using a bat or a racket is a gross motor skill

▲ Grasping a pencil is a fine motor skill

Basic stages of physical development	
Age	**Stage of development**
0–3 months	Infant will start to have control of head.
3–6 months	Babies will start to roll from side to side and push themselves up with their arms when on their front.
6–9 months	Babies start to grasp objects and sit unsupported. They may start to move by trying to crawl or shuffle.
9–12 months	Babies will have started to crawl or even walk. Starting to reach for objects.
1–2 years	Starting to build using blocks, make marks with a crayon, turn pages in picture books. Gaining confidence. Enjoying repetitive play and games and songs with a known outcome, for example 'Pat-a-cake' or 'Round and round the garden'.
2–3 years	Uses a spoon, puts on shoes, begins to use a preferred hand. Walks up and down stairs with confidence.
3–4 years	Turns pages in a book, puts on coat and shoes, throws and kicks a ball, washes and dries hands with help.
4–5 years	Draws a person, cuts out simple shapes, completing simple puzzles, starting to hop.
5–6 years	Forms letters, writes name, dresses and undresses, runs quickly, uses large apparatus.
6–7 years	Handwriting evenly spaced, ties laces, can complete more complex puzzles, chases and plays with others.
7–11 years	Refining physical skills such as running, jumping and skipping.

▲ Look at the photos of the children. One is 2 and the other is 4. What are they doing? How much physical progress can you see?

Physical needs of children in the Early Years

When children first arrive in your care, the majority will have developed a number of physical skills. These will have been developed through a range of physical activities which they have will have experienced by this age, for example walking, running, riding tricycles for their gross motor skills and holding a knife and fork or a pencil, for fine motor skills. Children will need to have opportunities to develop these skills within the learning environment through a selection of indoor and outdoor activities.

The kinds of activities which may be used within the early years to promote physical development	
Gross motor skills:	running, skipping, balancing, riding a bicycle, throwing and catching a ball.
Fine motor skills:	threading, painting, sand and water play, simple handwriting skills, cutting with scissors, puzzles.

Social and emotional development

The social and emotional development of children is directly linked to the way in which they begin to relate to others. Children need to interact with others so that they have opportunities to gain confidence. Children who are well-developed socially and emotionally will be able to communicate with confidence, make their needs known and avoid becoming frustrated.

The main stages of social and emotional development are as follows:

Stages of social and emotional development	
Age	**Stage of development**
0–12 months	Babies start to communicate through smiling and making eye contact with their families. They will enjoy being cuddled and played with.
1–2 years	Children start to gain a sense of their own identities. They will respond to their own names and start to explore independently. They will start to show anger if their needs are not met and do not yet recognise the needs of others. This is sometimes called the 'terrible twos'. Children start to play with others.
2–3 years	Children will start to show concern for others but will still have strong feelings about their own needs being met. They will be starting to come to terms with their own independence.
3–4 years	This is a more settled year and children will be growing in confidence and social skills. They may still have tantrums as they will still feel strong emotions, but will be starting to play independently for longer periods.
4–6 years	Children will generally feel much more confident in themselves and start to be proud of their own achievements. Close friendships are increasingly more important to them.

Stages of social and emotional development (cont.)	
Age	**Stage of development**
6–8 years	Children start to develop a sense of fairness and are more able to share items and equipment. They have a greater self-awareness and can be critical of themselves. They may start to compare themselves to their peers. Friendship groups can start to be problematic if children fall out with one another. Children will also make some gender friendships in this age group.
8–11 years	Children will be settled in their friendships and may form more stable 'groups'. They will continue to compare themselves with others and will need to 'belong'.

If children have specific needs, for example a hearing disability, then this may affect the way in which they develop overall. For example, if they cannot hear or communicate clearly they may not be able to join in and can become withdrawn. It is particularly important for children's development that any special needs are identified early and that the necessary support is put into place.

Children who are entering school will be at an age where they are just beginning to gain confidence and become independent. They will still be developing their ability to show desirable behaviour and will be learning how to share and think of other people. As an adult working with young children, you need to give children as many

▲ Children must develop a good self-image in order to fulfil their potential

opportunities as possible to allow them to feel independent and to praise them as much as they can for good behaviour. In this way, children will start to develop a positive *self-esteem*. Self-esteem is how we feel about ourselves and the image we have of ourselves. Children develop a positive self-esteem when they feel good about themselves and when they feel valued. The way in which we treat children has a direct effect on this so it is important that we encourage and praise them, value each one as an individual and celebrate differences and similarities.

The rate at which a child will develop socially and emotionally will depend on the opportunities which have been given for them to interact with others. For example where a child has come from a large family, there may have been many more opportunities to play with others and form relationships. If a child has had very little contact or social interaction with other children, it may be more difficult, when starting at a school or nursery, to understand how relationships with others are formed.

Case study

David is an only child of older parents. Although he has been to playgroup 2 mornings a week, his mother has always been with him, so he has never had experience of being away from her. He has one friend, Neil, who has started at another school.

Flora is the youngest of 5 children. She comes from a big extended family and has often been looked after by her older siblings, aunts or cousins. She is lively and outgoing and determined not to be left behind in anything.

1 How might David and Flora behave when they first arrive in Reception?

2 In what ways are David's and Flora's needs different?

3 What kind of support might each child need when settling into class.

Discuss in pairs.

Knowledge into action

Ask your mentor or class teacher whether you can observe 2 different children within a class. Look at the way they interact with other children. Do you think this is 'normal' for their ages and stages of development?

Intellectual development

Children's learning is based on their own individual experiences and personalities and although they will pass through different stages in their learning, the age at which they reach them is not fixed. All children will develop at their own pace and in their own way and will have their own learning requirements. Factors which will affect their learning will include:

▷ motivation – the child's desire to learn and their interest in a task

▷ social background – how much the child has mixed with others and the kinds of experiences they have had outside the home

▷ emotional factors – whether the child's home life has been happy and settled

▷ intelligence and creativity – the child's own aptitudes and talents

▷ age and maturity – how mature the child is for his or her age

▷ ability to concentrate – the child's ability and willingness to concentrate on a task.

Factors which may affect children's behaviour

There are a number of factors which will have an effect on the way in which chidren behave.

Background

Children will enter schools with a variety of backgrounds and experiences, all of which will have affected the way in which their individual personalities react to others. Some children may come from a secure and loving family background while others may have had very unsettled experiences or a series of different homes and carers. Some may

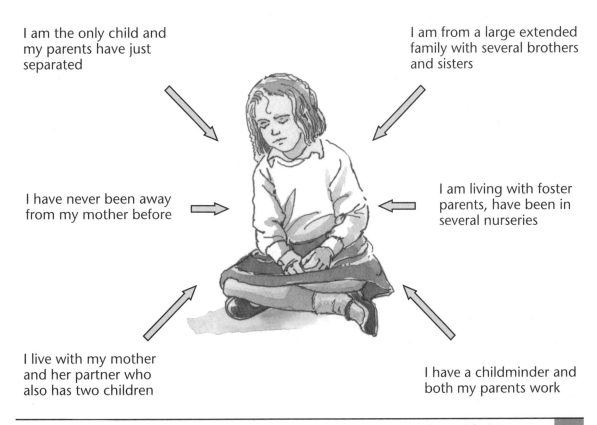

I am the only child and my parents have just separated

I am from a large extended family with several brothers and sisters

I have never been away from my mother before

I am living with foster parents, have been in several nurseries

I live with my mother and her partner who also has two children

I have a childminder and both my parents work

have experienced many social situations while others' experience may be limited to family members or friends. These experiences will affect the child's ability and confidence when socialising with others.

There will also be other factors which will have an effect on the way in which children behave:

Age

The child may develop physically or socially particularly quickly or slowly for their age. This can affect the way that others see them which in turn will impact on their behaviour. For example, a child who is particularly small for his or her age may have been 'babied' at home and may find it difficult when faced with the need for increasing independence.

Gender

It may be that a child enters school with limited experiences due to gender, for example parents who have not allowed a boy to experience sewing or cooking. As a result of this, the child may not expect that both sexes may be able to participate in all tasks at school.

Medical

A child who was premature at birth may have delayed physical development and this can also be the cause of immature behaviour. Some children who have medical intervention for specific problems such as poor hearing may be less confident about becoming involved with tasks within the classroom. At an early age, some physical problems may be as yet undiagnosed so it is important to be aware that these children may not be picking up on various cues or be aware of what is expected of them.

Special needs

It is now a statutory requirement to encourage the inclusion into mainstream schools of children with special needs. According to the Disability Discrimination Act (1995), a person has a disability if 'he or she has a physical or mental impairment that has a substantial and long-term adverse effect on his or her ability to carry out normal day to day activities.' The inclusion of disabled pupils is to encourage more positive integration of disabled people into society and to give children a greater understanding of the needs of others. The impact of recent legislation called the Special Needs Code of Practice means that there are now more children with special needs in mainstream schools.

Culture

Children may enter school from a variety of cultures. Some of these may encourage particular behaviours from men and women which differ from those in school. For example, some cultures may not encourage women to go out to work. In early years settings, teachers and assistants are predominantly female which some children may find strange.

Self-esteem

All children's self-esteem, or how they view themselves, is directly affected by whether they feel valued by others. A child whose self-esteem is low may display behaviours which are disruptive or may also withdraw and be timid in class. There may be several reasons why a child has low self-esteem. These could include poor relationships at home or a family who spends little time with the child.

 Case study

Richard has been in school for a year. He is very able orally but has trouble with recording his ideas, as his written work is not of the same level as that of his peers. He often starts trying to write things down and quickly becomes frustrated, saying that his work is no good and wanting to tear it up and start again.

1 Why do you think Richard might say that his work is no good?

2 How might the class teacher and assistant help to improve Richard's self-esteem?

Stereotyping

'Stereotyping' means expecting certain things of different people. The comment 'boys are always noisier than girls' is stereotyping. When you work with children, you need to also be aware of their own assumptions and opinions about pupils' behaviour relative to these factors. For example, stereotyping of children when giving them tasks within the school. 'I need some sensible girls to go on this message for me' may sound to the boys that only girls can be sensible. Care should also be taken in other situations: it should not be assumed that a child with a disability is unable to take part in actvities – they should be included wherever possible.

 Knowledge into action

What measures does your school have in place so that stereotyping of different groups is avoided? Do you think that children come into school with particular ideas about the kinds of activities girls and boys might do? Give a reason for your answer.

Learning difficulties or inappropriate task given

If a child feels unable to complete a task, poor behaviour may result as they will not be able to focus their attention on the activity. This may be due to the teacher giving the child an inappropriate task for his ability, but could also be due to an undiagnosed learning difficulty.

Behaviour patterns which may indicate problems

Learning how to behave is an important part of a child's development. This is because it is a learned skill which affects the way in which they will interact with others. Children must learn to be able to listen to others, take turns, share and show good manners. Otherwise they may find that they become isolated or are disliked and rejected by other children. Some children may enter schools with less experience than others and need to have more guidance from staff.

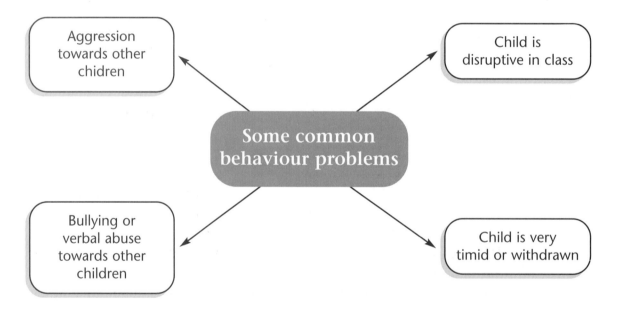

▲ Behaviour problems can take different forms

Children may start to show signs of behaviour which is significantly different from that of other children immediately or it may not become apparent until later.

▷ **Child is timid or withdrawn** This kind of behaviour may be shyness and some children may take some time to settle into new surroundings, especially if they have had an unsettled home life. However, children will usually start to make friends and join in with activities fairly quickly, even if they remain shy with adults. If a child is very timid with parents but not within the setting, staff should be aware that this could be an indication of problems at home or even of child abuse.

▲ Assistants will need to be aware if a child is not settling in with others

▷ **Child is very disruptive in the class** This could take the form of calling out or disturbing other children. It can be caused by the child seeking attention from adults within the setting. This may be because the child receives a lot of attention at home and has become used to it. Children who do not receive much attention from adults at home may also resort to being disruptive, even though the attention they will receive is negative.

▷ **Child is aggressive towards other children** This may be another attention seeking device or the child may not have had many social experiences with other children before starting school. It takes time for children to learn social skills such as turn-taking and sharing with others. Some children take longer to adapt to waiting their turn and being one of a group and may find it difficult.

▷ **Child bullies others** Bullying can be either physical or verbal and can be over a period of time, possibly leading to the victim being reluctant to come to school. The bully will feel a need to have control over others, perhaps because of their own insecurities. A child may use verbal abuse to others including racist/sexist/religious comments, personal abuse or bad language. This is not common at an early age but it does happen within primary schools. Some children may have heard some verbal abuse at home or on television and use it on others, copying poor role models. It is important that such behaviour is challenged and that positive role modelling occurs within all schools.

Children who have been abused

Children may display behaviour which indicates that they have been abused in some way. Abuse can be physical, emotional, sexual or caused by neglect. A child could also be the victim of more than one of these.

Examples of behaviour which may give cause for concern:

▷ Child is reluctant to change for PE or remove clothing. Whilst this is perfectly normal for some children it may also be a sign that the child has been the victim of physical abuse and is aware that the abuse will be visible. Look out for marks, bruises or burns which may not be caused by accident. Look for bruising or marks which may form a pattern, for example hand shaped.

▷ Child displays uncharacteristic behaviour patterns from those normally shown. If a child suddenly starts to behave very differently and is particularly 'clingy' with adults or is reluctant to go home, this should be reported to the adult in charge of the class. This may indicate physical, emotional or sexual abuse.

▷ Child is unusually tearful or attention seeking. Where parents or carers emotionally abuse a child, the child may become insecure and need more attention.

▷ Inappropriate sexual behaviour. This may be shown in different ways, but children may display behaviour which is uncharacteristic at their age, for example using language of which they should not be aware or pestering other children by looking at them or touching them inappropriately.

You may also find yourself in the position of suspecting that a child has been subjected or exposed to some form of substance abuse. This could be through parents or older brothers and sisters. The main indicators would be health and emotional problems or the child may not relate to others, either children or staff, as before.

Where adults have any suspicion of child abuse or neglect, they should immediately inform the teacher or supervisor with whom they are working. In this way, steps can be taken to monitor the child and keep a record of any signs of abuse. When recording

Case study

Melissa has always behaved well at school although she is extremely quiet and has not socialised much with other children or adults. She has recently started to become more interested in the group and mix more freely with the others although she is still reluctant to talk to adults. When her mother comes to collect her from school one day, she says that she does not want to go home.

1 Why might Melissa have initially been so shy to join the class?

2 Discuss in your group what you might do if this happened to a child with whom you are working.

incidents, note should be taken of the child's name, any other child involved, the date and the exact behaviour shown. It is also important to reassure and listen to children if they are able to talk about what has happened to them, whilst taking care not to make promises to not tell anyone else or keep secrets (more on how and when to report in section 3-1.2).

School policies for rewarding positive behaviour and managing unwanted behaviour

Theories about behaviour

There are three main theories about behaviour and how children learn.

▷ **Social learning theory,** developed by Albert Bandura in the 1960s, suggests that children will learn by copying the behaviour of those around them. They will tend to copy adults, and later their peers. This means that it is important that children have good role models for behaviour so that they learn appropriate behaviour themselves.

What this means for the adult: Adults should remember that they will be teaching children not only by what they say, but also by what they do. Where a child sees an adult being courteous and kind to others, it will encourage them to behave in the same way. Similarly, if a child usually witnesses loud or aggressive behaviour, they will learn that this is the way to behave. Adults should therefore remember that they need to be good *role models* for children.

▷ **Behaviourist theory,** developed by Skinner in the 1940s, suggests that children will respond to praise and so will repeat behaviour which gives them recognition or praise for what they do. This kind of praise may take the form of rewards such as stickers, charts or adult attention. Children who receive praise or attention for positive behaviour such as kindness towards others are more likely to repeat this behaviour.

What this means for the adult: Adults need to remember to praise positive behaviour wherever possible, as children will also try to get their attention through undesirable behaviour. Where we can, we should ignore this kind of behaviour and instead give attention to those children who are behaving well.

▷ Another view widely held in psychology is the **Self-fulfilling prophecy theory**, which states that children will be influenced by the way in which adults think about them. Children want to be noticed by adults and approved of. In this way, when adults believe a child is 'good', their opinion will encourage and influence the behaviour of that child. If adults think that a child is 'naughty', the child will live up to this expectation.

What this means for the adult: When speaking to children about their behaviour, we should always label the behaviour rather than the individual, for example 'That was a silly thing to do,' rather than 'What a silly girl you are'.

On the first day of term, you are helping the new children into a Reception class. One of the mothers says to you, in front of her child, 'This is Natalie – you will need to watch her because she is a naughty girl'.

How do you think this will make Natalie feel?

What sort of behaviour might Natalie display?

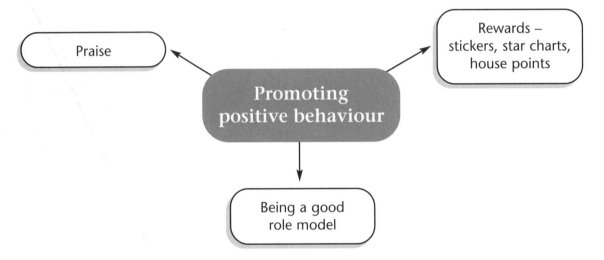

▲ Promoting positive behaviour can take different forms

Strategies for promoting positive behaviour

Adults need to remember that young children need to be praised for work and behaviour genuinely and frequently for effort and achievement. This will reinforce good behaviour and build self-esteem.

Schools may vary in what they do to promote good behaviour, but as with strategies for managing poor behaviour, this should be consistent throughout the school. Ways in which the school promotes good behaviour may be through whole school programmes of rewards such as house points, or for younger children, smiley faces or charts for

> **Class RB We have followed our class rules**
> Blue group ☺ ☺ ☺
> Red group ☺ ☺
> Yellow group ☺ ☺ ☺ ☺
> Green group ☺ ☺ ☺ ☺

▲ How might this chart be motivating for children?

▲ Assistants can help by having positive relationships with children

groups who are behaving well. Usually children will also respond very well to occasionally being sent to another member of staff if they have done something particularly well, for example their previous teacher or the deputy or head.

In any early years setting, it is important to manage children's behaviour well so that their learning takes place in an effective environment. All adults within the setting should have high expectations so that a pattern of positive behaviour is established. Children need to be aware of what these expectations are, and there should be a behaviour management policy in the school with consistent adult expectations.

It is imperative in any childcare setting for children to be aware of a set of rules or guidelines so that they have a clear understanding of how to behave. Children need to be aware of the boundaries within which to behave so that they understand what is expected of them.

Hawkwood Infant School

<u>Golden Rules</u>

1. I will treat myself and others with respect at all times.
2. I will treat all property with respect at all times.
3. I will play fair and friendly games in the playground.
4. I will work hard and always try to do my best.
5. I will walk quietly around the school.

Mountfield Infant School
Behaviour Management Policy

At Mountfield school we believe that all children should be guided by a positive and professional approach to behaviour. This should be fairly and consistently applied by all adults (teachers, assistants, students, midday supervisors) who may have cause to discipline a child. It should establish the hierarchy for dealing with problems within school.

To work well, this policy must have the support of all members of the community, including the children, and should therefore be developed by them as a whole and be based on professional agreement. We have endeavoured to do this. This document therefore needs to be read and understood by all governors, teaching and support staff and midday supervisors.

Aims

The main aim of this policy is to help us to create an environment in which effective learning takes place. It should make us aware of the part our responses play in establishing a pattern of positive behaviour based on high expectations and mutual respect.

It aims to inform children, parents, governors and all teaching and support staff of our high standards and expresses our shared understanding of how we expect children to behave. It aims to inform all concerned of effective strategies that can be used to encourage positive behaviour and advise as to the consequences of misbehaviour.

We will expect all children to know, understand and adhere to our school rules.

Objectives

The staff at our school will be encouraged to:

- ▶ Have a professional approach at all times
- ▶ Provide well structured environments to avoid disputes
- ▶ Create a working environment where children are able to achieve and where their work is seen to be valued
- ▶ Have high but realistic expectations of work and behaviour
- ▶ Praise work and behaviour frequently to reinforce good behaviour
- ▶ Be polite at all times to children and other adults to increase mutual respect and trust
- ▶ See parents as active partners and build positive relationships
- ▶ Make our expectations of work clear and consistent, ensuring our instructions are understood
- ▶ Intervene early so that misbehaviour does not escalate
- ▶ Be seen to be fair – try to establish all the facts

▲ First page of a school's Behaviour Policy

These rules should be written in such a way that the children are given positive targets, for example 'I will walk quietly around the school' rather than negative, for example 'Do not run in school'. Where the language may be difficult for young children to understand, for example 'treating others with respect', it should be clear that they understand its meaning. The rules should be discussed frequently with the children both in class and during assembly times so that they understand and remember them.

As well as this list of school rules, pupils should be encouraged to behave in a positive way through watching the behaviour of adults. A child will soon notice if an adult is not acting in a way that they would expect or there are not consistent expectations between adults. When a child is behaving particularly well, adults should remember to praise this behaviour so that it is recognised.

 Case study

You have been asked to work with a small group of children to make a Father's Day card. You have all the materials you need and have started to work on the cards but notice that 2 children in your group are not paying attention and are distracting the others.

1 How might you draw attention to the fact that some of the group are working well?

2 What might you do to promote the good behaviour which you have in the group? What would you say to the children who are not on task?

Where there are cases of unwanted behaviour, staff will need to be familiar with the school's behaviour policy (see page 160) so that their responses and strategies tie in with whole school policy.

Using sanctions to manage behaviour

In any early years setting or school, staff will need a scale of agreed sanctions to use for managing unwanted behaviour. They may even have their own classroom rules for behaviour, which the children can devise themselves with a little help. In this way, children will be able to take responsibility for their own behaviour and understand the results of their actions. Where children are showing unwanted behaviour, it is important for staff to know when to intervene, especially where children are a danger to themselves or others. Depending on the age of the children and the situation (for example in the dining hall, classroom, playground and so on) the scale of sanctions may vary, but children should be aware of them.

Sent to
Headteacher
↑
Sent to Deputy Head
teacher
↑
Sent to Year group leader/Head of Year
↑
Miss part of playtime – child is kept in
and/or asked to write a letter of apology
↑
Time out – child is removed from the situation
↑
Verbal warning – child is told that their behaviour
has been noted and that they will be given time out the next time

▲ Example of a scale of sanctions to manage unwanted behaviour

▲ It is not always possible to ignore bad behaviour

Keys to good practice
Managing unwanted behaviour

✔ Intervene early so that the problem does not escalate. If a situation arises where an assistant is the first to be aware of unacceptable behaviour, such as children misbehaving in the playground, it would be appropriate to draw the teacher's attention to it or if this is not possible, to intervene.

✔ Give eye contact to the child who is misbehaving. Sometimes all that is needed is a stern look at a child so that they see an adult is aware of what they are doing.

✔ Remove items which are being used inappropriately. If a child is using an item, for example a pair of scissors or a piece of outdoor equipment, to hurt another child, these should be gently taken away. The child should then be told why they have been removed and when they will be able to have them back.

✔ Proximity – move closer to a child who is misbehaving so that they are aware of an adult presence. This will usually prevent the behaviour from continuing. Assistants can use this practice in whole class teaching time when the teacher is at the front to calm or prevent inappropriate behaviour by having an awareness of who to sit beside.

✔ Time out – this is sometimes used when older children are consistently misbehaving and need to be given some time to calm down before returning to a situation. It can be applied within the classroom or in the playground.

✔ Use a scale of sanctions which the children are aware of, for example:

    a time out

    b miss one minute or longer of playtime

    c send to Deputy Head

    d send to Headteacher/speak to parents.

Your role and responsibilities and those of others when managing behaviour in school

As a teaching assistant, you will need to be aware of your role within the school for managing children's behaviour. If you have any worries or concerns about how to deal with children's behaviour you must always refer to the class teacher or supervisor. They will have the ultimate responsibility for managing behaviour of children within the class and the head teacher has responsibility for all the children within the school. The school's behaviour policy will offer guidelines and school strategies for dealing with behaviour.

Some of the responsibilities of staff should include:

▷ Having high but realistic expectations of work and behaviour. Children should be aware of how they should behave and praised when they do. Adults need to give praise such as 'I know how sensibly you can sit on the carpet for a story' rather than 'This class never sits quietly for a story'.

▷ Creating a working environment where children can achieve and where their work and efforts are seen to be valued, thus developing their self esteem. This can be done verbally as well as through displays of children's work and by sharing with other children and adults in the school.

▷ Making expectations of behaviour and work clear and consistent and ensuring instructions have been understood. If children are unsure of what they need to do, it is very difficult for them to automatically behave in a way which adults expect.

▷ Working consistently as a staff so that the same expectations apply throughout the school. This is vital so that the children understand that all staff are working together throughout the school.

▷ Being aware of your own values and opinions. You should ensure that you do not make assumptions about people on the grounds of gender, race or disability.

Evidence collection

Simulation may be used to obtain evidence in relation to recognition of uncharacteristic behaviour patterns and incidents of inappropriate behaviour outside your area of responsibility.

Speak to your mentor about your school's Behaviour Policy.

▶ Discuss the school's strategies for managing unwanted behaviour.

▶ Find out how the school ensures that all staff are aware of these strategies.

▶ Note it down and keep it as evidence of your learning.

School policies and practices for children with emotional and behavioural needs

Your school may have a range of strategies in place for supporting children who have emotional or behavioural difficulties. As discussed in Unit 3-1, the strategies you may need to use with these children should be those which are used by the whole school. It is important that children are aware of the consequences of their actions and why these sanctions are necessary.

School policies which relate to **children's emotional development** may include:

▷ behaviour policy – this will give staff strategies and guidelines when managing behaviour in school

▷ PSHE policy – this will give details of the way in which staff carry out the National Curriculum with regard to personal, social and health education

▷ inclusion and equal opportunities policies – these policies will promote the school's ethos and procedures in these two areas

▷ anti-bullying policy – since September 1999, schools have been legally required to implement anti-bullying policies

▷ child protection policy – this will have an effect on the way staff are alert at all times for signs of abuse or neglect in children. It will give you an indication of the key points which you need to observe and the person you need to go to in order to report any concerns

▷ schools are also now required to have a clear anti-racism policy.

You will need to know the range of strategies the school uses to diffuse and manage children's emotions.

In your class, you may find that the class teacher uses various strategies for managing negative emotions. Circle time is often used in classrooms although it is not always appropriate for very young children, as they need to sit for a long time to wait for their turn.

Staff will need to know how to recognise the types of activities which will encourage the expression of feelings and emotions. As an assistant, you should be able to support children and encourage them to express and discuss how they are feeling. You will need to be:

▷ **observant** – make sure you are always looking out for pupils. The class teacher may not be aware of a child who has been particularly quiet – but this could be a sign that there is a problem. There may also be a child who is behaving in a different way from usual, for example, is short tempered or seeking attention.

▷ **approachable** – if children feel comfortable with you and relaxed, they are more likely to come to you if they have a problem or are upset. They may also want to tell you about something good that has happened which is making them feel

---

Teaching tip: Make sure you don't appear to favour only one child.

▲ There are different strategies for helping children to manage negative emotions

positive. You will need to try to develop good relationships with all children over time, through being interested and listening to what they have to say.

▷ **aware of confidentiality issues** – you must be aware that any information about a child is confidential and you should not discuss any issues outside the school environment. The school will also have policies and procedures for ensuring confidentiality, by making sure that computer passwords and files on children are only seen by those who are authorised to read them. Alternatively, a child with an emotional problem may approach you, or you may feel that they need to discuss something which is upsetting them with an adult. In this situation you will need to tell the child before they confide in you that you cannot guarantee that you will not tell another adult, for example, if a child is being harmed in any way.

▷ **possible causes of children's negative outbursts and reactions** – there is a variety of reasons that children may have negative outbursts or react in an uncharacteristic

Possible reasons for negative reactions by children

Bullying – the child may have been bullied intermittently for periods since they have been in school. They may be reluctant to tell staff as they are unsure of the response.

Inability to cope with academic work – the child may be finding that they cannot manage their work and need to have extra support or may be diagnosed as having special educational needs. This may be difficult for the child to manage emotionally.

Divorce or separation in family – the child may be angry with either parent or unable to express their emotions. They may also blame themselves for what has happened.

New baby – this may cause a child to feel insecure and need more attention. If this is not given at home, the child may try to gain attention in school.

Death or illness in family – this will upset the child and could cause outbursts or regressive behaviour, such as withdrawing or thumb-sucking.

Changing class or school – this may cause pupils to feel insecure and unsure about where they fit in with other children.

Substance abuse – children may seem to be detached and show signs of neglect or tiredness.

Sexual abuse – this may cause mood swings and changes in behaviour. The child may behave differently with other children or adults.

Physical abuse – children who are being physically abused may be nervous or jumpy around adults. They may find it difficult to trust adults and could be quiet or withdrawn and lack self-esteem.

Verbal abuse – children who are verbally abused may be very quiet and may also have low self-esteem.

Change in carer – this will have a disruptive influence on the child's home life and could affect their self-esteem as they may feel rejected. Children may become detached from others because of a fear of this happening again.

Moving house – this may be difficult if children need to start at a new school and form new relationships. Even moving home within the same area can be hard for some children.

way. It is important that staff are aware of the different factors that can have an effect on children's behaviour.

Any of these factors may make it difficult for a child to manage their behaviour and emotions in school. Assistants will need to voice any concerns they have about particular children to others within the school.

Problems when dealing with children who have emotional difficulties

You may find that pupils are the victims of cultural or gender stereotypes and are not freely able to talk about their feelings as they are not encouraged to at home. Some parents may not feel that boys, for example, should be able to discuss how they feel but should 'put a brave face on it.' This may limit the child's emotional development and make it difficult for them to bring their feelings into the open. If this is the case, you will need to be understanding and reassure them that it is acceptable to talk about feelings and emotions rather than keep them hidden.

When pupils are not able to express how they feel, there may be problems later and behavioural problems could arise, especially if pupils become frustrated by their inability to discuss their feelings.

Keys to good practice
Managing pupils' emotions

✔ Form good relationships with pupils.

✔ Look for any signs of distress/unusual behaviour.

✔ Always remain calm and reassure pupils.

✔ Be aware of confidentiality issues.

How to work in line with local and national guidelines and policies

It is useful to be aware of how your school's policies fit in with local guidelines and policies. You may need to ask other members of staff when the Behaviour policy was devised and whether they used a borough model or local guidelines.

The DFES induction training for behaviour management for assistants outlines some core principles to help those who are working with children. Some of these are to:

▷ plan for good behaviour

▷ work within the 4 R's framework: Rules, Routines, Responsibilities and Rights

▷ separate the (inappropriate) behaviour from the child

▷ use the language of choice

▷ actively build trust and rapport

▷ model the behaviour that you want to see

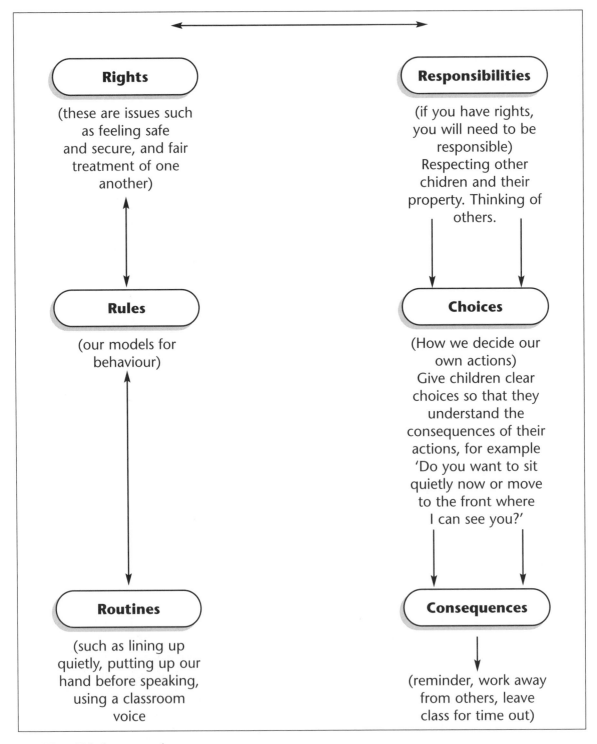

▲ The 4R's framework

As can be seen, these fit in with the types of ground rules which are expected of children in most schools. Children will need to be aware of others' expectations of them and how they fit into the school as a whole. These guidelines give the choice to the individual as well as an awareness of the consequences of their actions.

Knowledge into action

Take the 6 headings in the 4R's framework and write down some examples of each. Discuss them in your group. How far do you think children are aware of the consequences of their actions?

Element 3-1.2 Support the implementation of strategies to manage pupil behaviour

For this element, you will need to know and understand the following:

▶ managing behaviour and the implications of the Children Act and child protection

▶ reporting behaviour or discipline problems to the teacher and procedures for doing this

▶ specialist advice which is available within and outside school for dealing with unwanted behaviour

▶ implementing behaviour support plans for individual children

Managing behaviour and the implications of The Children Act 1989 and child protection

When looking at behaviour which is acceptable, adults should be aware that we all have different ideas and expectations. We should recognise that our ideas about what is acceptable or unacceptable will come from our own experiences and cultures. Children may therefore enter schools and nurseries with a variety of accepted 'normal' behaviour.

We may therefore have conflicting ideas about the kind of behaviour we view as 'normal' and which we expect from children. For this reason, many schools and nurseries will have their own guidelines for behaviour (see page 157). Parents should be informed of these so that they are aware of what is acceptable and not acceptable in school. Where parents and schools have conflicting ideas about acceptable behaviour, children will find it difficult to know how to conform.

? Think about it

Think about the following statements:

▶ children should always write 'thank you letters' at Christmas and birthdays

▶ children should never leave the table until everyone has finished eating

▶ children should be required to fast during Ramadan

▶ children should always stand up when an adult enters the room

▶ children should not be allowed to address an adult by their first name.

Which of these statements do you agree with?

Do others in the room give the same answers as you?

As already mentioned, children should be aware and reminded of the school's expectations for behaviour so that they know how to conform in the classroom, playground and in other parts of the school. Where children are not conforming to the rules, they should know what the consequences are.

 Find out about...

The rules in your school. How does the school remind the children about them?

Examples of behaviour and consequences	
Action	**Consequence**
Running in the school corridor	Going back and walking
Disruptive behaviour in class	Time out – working alone
Verbally abusing other children/adults	Apology/letter of apology
Aggressive behaviour in the playground	One minute by the wall

The school's policies on behaviour and equal opportunities should set out guidelines for managing the way in which pupils interact with one another. Where assistants are unsure of the kinds of sanctions or consequences that they are able to use, they should always clarify this with their class teacher or supervisor.

The Children Act (1989)

This Act was passed in 1989 and has had far reaching effects on the care and protection of children. It aims to make professionals and local authorities dealing with

▲ It is important to encourage good behaviour but sanctions may still be necessary

families and children think about their individual needs. The Children Act covers a wide range of issues including the registration and inspection of childcare services for children under 8. It also provides guidance for child protection issues and should therefore be considered when selecting and using behaviour management strategies.

All children who are placed in situations of care should be protected and the Act outlines the responsibilities of the local authority in ensuring that these needs are met. Where schools and nurseries are looking after young children it is important for all staff to know and understand the rights of children and how they should be protected, for example that adults are not allowed to give corporal punishment. It is through the school's policies and guidelines for behaviour management that inspectors can see that all staff are aware of and adhere to these guidelines. Behaviour management strategies will need to take into consideration how we can encourage good behaviour and remain fair when applying sanctions for bad behaviour.

The Human Rights Act which was amended in 2002 further emphasises the rights of all people, children included, to be treated with respect and as an individual.

Reporting behaviour or discipline problems to the teacher and procedures for doing this

Working alongside the teacher to promote an effective learning environment

When working in partnership with the class teacher, assistants should be clear about their roles and responsibilities with regard to pupil behaviour. This is as important for adults in the school to know and understand as it is for children, since they are responsible for ensuring that school policies and rules for behaviour are maintained.

> ▶ National guidelines for behaviour management
> ▶ Local guidelines
> ▶ School behaviour policy
> ▶ School rules
> ▶ Class rules
> ▶ Playground rules
> ▶ Rules for using the computer room/cooking room/apparatus in the hall/working in the school grounds/safety on school visits

▲ Structure of the way in which rules are defined

Assistants may find it difficult to know when and how they should intervene when they are faced with issues of behaviour. It is important to be clear exactly what 'normal' behaviour is and to make allowances for children in different circumstances. Some examples of these might be:

▷ On the first day of a new school, there may be several children who are upset and do not want to leave their parent or carer. However, if this behaviour carried on over a long period of time, the teacher may find it necessary to impose some kind of strategy for managing the child or children.

▷ It is getting towards the end of term and the normal routines of school are slightly different due to end of term activities. The children in the class are very excitable and restless. In this situation, which is not normal, some children may find it difficult to conform to the rules.

▷ There has been a Book Week in school. The children have been able to meet authors and have seen a small play. They are finding it difficult to sit still and listen when they go back to class.

Teachers and assistants should also be informed if a child in the class has had any kinds of upheaval or distress at home. The teacher should inform any assistants as soon as a problem comes to his or her attention. Examples of these might be a divorce or a death in the family. Sometimes it may be the death of a pet, or a parent going away on business which can make a child behave differently. The school should make it clear to parents that staff need to be informed of anything which may be distressing the child. If assistants notice a child behaving differently or out of character, this is worth mentioning to the teacher so that parents can be asked if there is any reason for it. When children are settled in school and used to the rules and routines, they will know and understand what is expected of them. Where children display unwanted behaviour in a normal school situation, sanctions should be applied to control the behaviour.

Applying sanctions

As a teaching assistant, you should be aware of the types of sanctions or rewards which are available to you when managing behaviour. Usually if the teacher is present, your main strategies will be verbal or involve eye contact. If you are alone with the class for any reason you should, as the responsible adult, be able to use any of those which the teacher would normally use. However, you should always clarify this with the teacher first. If you have any problems in implementing sanctions or if the children do not respond to you as the responsible adult, you should also inform the teacher. If sanctions are applied and the child is still consistently not responding, there may be a deep-rooted problem which should be investigated. (see page 174 for specialist advice on behaviour management)

Case study

You have been left with the class for 10 minutes as the teacher has had to speak to the headteacher urgently. You are reading the class a story but 2 or 3 girls at the back are not listening and are disturbing the others. You tell them to behave sensibly and listen to the story but one of them says that you are not the teacher and they don't have to do what you say.

1 What would you do in this situation?

2 What could the teacher say to the class before leaving to make sure that they behaved appropriately?

3 Discuss with your mentor how you think the class teacher could support you.

Safety Issues

Other situations in which you may need to apply sanctions or strategies are those when you find yourself or others at risk. It is important to be able to respond calmly and quickly in emergencies and other potentially dangerous situations. This may occur either within the school and grounds or on a school trip.

Examples of this could be:

▷ a child or parent who becomes violent

▷ a child who unwittingly puts others in danger

▷ a child who displays severe behavioural problems and needs full adult attention

▷ a group of children who are misbehaving and putting others in danger.

If you find yourself in a situation where there is no other adult present and you are faced with a risk, you will be responsible for managing the situation. You must always remain calm, as children will quickly panic if they sense this in an adult. If it is a single child who is misbehaving or violent and they do not respond to your authority, you must make sure that other children are kept away from them and send a responsible child for another adult. Similarly, when faced with an adult who is aggressive or violent, remain calm and reassure them that you will need to ask for assistance from another member of staff. It is important that you seek adult help as soon as possible.

Specialist advice which is available inside and outside school for dealing with unwanted behaviour

Where a teacher or supervisor has used all the ideas and strategies available to him or her, it may be necessary to ask for extra help and support. If you are in a mainstream school, you should have a SENCo, or Special Needs Co-ordinator, on the staff. In pre-school or nursery setting, there should also now be a SENCo to help co-ordinate outside help for children who need it. There may be different situations which require the help of outside agencies and as an assistant you will not be asked to contact them, but you should have an awareness of the support that is available.

▷ **SENCo** – this should be the first point of contact for behaviour support and devising additional strategies for use within the classroom. They will also contact other professionals outside the school.

▷ **Behaviour unit** – this unit is usually run by the local authority and will offer support and suggestions for dealing with pupils who have behaviour problems. They may also come into schools to observe or work with specific children.

▷ **Educational psychologists** – these professionals visit all schools regularly to support children and the adults who work with them. They offer help and advice on a variety of Special Needs problems, and may assess children and devise individual programmes. They are also involved with assessing those children who may need a statement of Special Educational Needs (see page 21).

Implementing behaviour support plans

The SENCo will be the first point of contact for teachers and with their help, teachers may devise an Individual Education Plan for children with learning difficulties or a Behaviour Support Plan for those who need it. This should set realistic targets for work or behaviour which should be Specific, Measurable, Achievable, Realistic and Time bound (SMART). It is vital that pupils have achievable targets, so that they are able to experience success and start to build positive behaviour. If you are an Individual Support Assistant and responsible for supporting a specific child in the class, it is likely that you are familiar with setting targets for the child with whom you are working.

Think about it

Look at the Behaviour Support Plan below. Ask your supervisor or mentor about the way in which targets are set for individual children. Discuss in your group how you could support the teacher when implementing this plan for a child in the class in which you are working. Think about the following during your discussion:

▶ understanding the strategies being used

▶ ensuring these are consistent between all staff

▶ recognising and responding appropriately to any risks to yourself or others when implementing the strategies

▶ reporting back any problems in implementing the strategies

▶ providing clear feedback on the effectiveness of the strategies and the progress made by the child.

At the review you, the class teacher and parent should discuss the success of any strategies used

No more than 3 targets – easier to achieve

Behaviour support plan

Name: James Fraser
Class: 1SW
Date set: March 2003   **Date for review:** May 2003

Targets: **Review:**

1. To sit close to the teacher when on the carpet to encourage him to listen carefully and prevent calling out.

James has stopped calling out although still finds it difficult to listen. Ongoing target.

2. To encourage good behaviour in the playground through teaching some playground games.

This has worked well – target achieved. Now teaching games to others.

Reviewed by: L Clark

The review column should contain comments and include next steps

▲ An example of a Behaviour support plan

Evidence collection

Working with your supervisor or mentor, look at the targets set for one individual child in your work setting. Discuss the strategies you might use to support the implementation of these targets. Write an account of your actions and keep a record for evidence.

End of unit test

1 What are the 3 main areas of children's development of which assistants should be aware?

2 At what age will most children be able to cut out simple shapes?

3 What is an example of a gross motor skill?

4 What kinds of factors will have an effect on the way in which children behave?

5 Name 3 common behaviour problems.

6 What kinds of behaviour might indicate that a child has been abused in some way?

7 What are 2 ways in which you can promote good behaviour within your school?

8 State 2 of the aims of the Children Act 1989.

9 What kinds of sanctions might you apply when a child is not conforming to expected behaviour?

10 What sources of specialist advice are available to schools and nurseries when dealing with unwanted behaviour?

References

CSIE, *Index for Inclusion* (2000)

DfEE, *Curriculum Guidance for the Foundation Stage* (QCA 2000)

Websites

CSIE: http://inclusion.uwe.ac.uk

QCA: www.qca.org.uk

Unit 3-10 Contribute to the maintenance of a safe and secure learning environment

There are two elements to this unit. These are:

3-10.1 Contribute to the maintenance of a safe and secure learning environment
3-10.2 Minimise the risks arising from health emergencies

In your role as a teaching assistant you will need to be aware of health and safety issues, both within the school and grounds and while visiting other places on school trips. Health and safety is a responsibility of all staff in the school and you will need to know the kinds of risks which may occur and to whom you need to report any safety issues.

If you are called upon to take action in the case of an emergency, you will need to know the level of assistance you should start to take and the kinds of action you should not. As any other responsible adult who is first on the scene, teaching assistants should always assess the situation and act accordingly. If they are trained in first aid, they should do what they can to remove any immediate danger to the casualty but wait for the first aider or emergency services to arrive.

Element 3-10.1 Contribute to the maintenance of a safe and secure learning environment

For this element, you will need to know and understand the following:

▶ school policies and procedures and your responsibilities within the school
▶ the types of health, safety and security risks which may occur
▶ appropriate action to take in an emergency.

School policies and procedures for health and safety and your responsibilities within the school

When you first start at a new school, you should have access to or be informed about the school's policy for health and safety. The Health and Safety at Work etc Act (1974) was designed to protect everyone at work through procedures for preventing accidents. The kinds of precautions all those in the workplace are expected to observe are:

To report any hazards

You will need to be alert to the kinds of hazards which are likely to cause injury to yourself and others in the school. The school is required to carry out an annual risk assessment to determine which areas and activities of the school are most likely to be hazardous, the

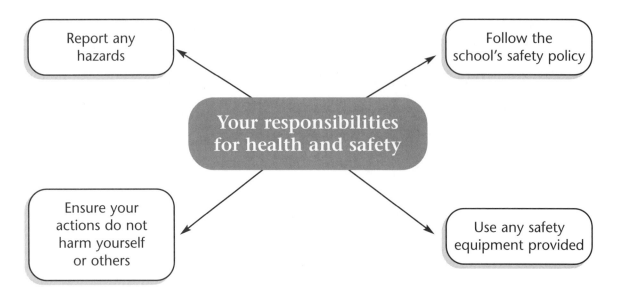

Report any hazards

Follow the school's safety policy

Your responsibilities for health and safety

Ensure your actions do not harm yourself or others

Use any safety equipment provided

▲ You must take responsibility for health and safety in the school

likelihood of this occurring and those who are at risk. Children and staff need to be vigilant and report any hazards which they notice immediately to the appropriate person. This may be the school's health and safety agent, the headteacher or another member of staff. You should be aware of the designated person to whom you should report health and safety matters (see pages 179 and 183 for the kinds of hazards which may occur).

To follow the school's safety policy

The school's policy should give information to all staff about procedures which the school has in place for ensuring that the school is as safe as possible and the school's guidance when dealing with health and safety issues. All new staff joining the school should be given induction training in safety procedures and what to do in case of emergencies. Safety should be a regular topic at staff and assistants' meetings.

 Knowledge into action

▶ Locate a copy of your health and safety policy.
▶ Find out about procedures for reporting accidents in your school.

To make sure that their actions do not harm themselves or others

Staff also need to ensure that any actions which they take are not likely to harm or cause a danger to others in the school. This will include tidying up and putting things away after use. It also includes taking no action when they discover a potential danger.

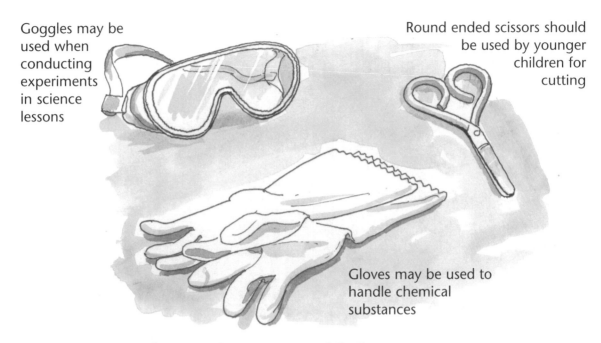

Goggles may be used when conducting experiments in science lessons

Round ended scissors should be used by younger children for cutting

Gloves may be used to handle chemical substances

To use any safety equipment provided

Staff will need to ensure that safety equipment which is provided for use when carrying out activities is always used. This will include safe use of tools which are used for subjects such as Design and Technology or gloves when handling materials in science activities. There should be guidelines in the school's policy for the safe use and storage of equipment.

All staff working within a school have a responsibility to ensure that children are cared for and safe. The Children Act (1989) also requires that we protect children as far as we can when they are in our care. This includes preventing any risks which may occur.

The types of health, safety and security risks which may occur

Internal hazards which may be found in schools

The table below shows some of the internal hazards which may be found in schools and the action to take for them.

Internal hazards	
Type of hazard (indoors)	**What to do**
Dangerous items left within children's reach (scissors, cleaning equipment and materials, kettles, hot drinks)	Remove or put away
Trailing electrical wires/overloaded plugs	Tidy, if possible or report
Untidy areas (things which can be tripped over	Tidy, if possible or report
Fire doors obstructed	Always keep clear

▲ See how many potential dangers you can find in this classroom

Schools should carry out regular checks to ensure that these types of risks are kept to a minimum and that staff are aware why they need to be vigilant and what to look for. Health and safety courses may be available to assistants who would like to have more training in this area. For more details of these, you should speak to your mentor.

There are also other materials and equipment used in schools which may present a risk if not used and stored correctly. Different stages or subject areas may use equipment and materials which are potentially hazardous to children or adults, although health and safety issues are relevant through all subject areas and all parts of the school:

 Find out about...

Who in your school is responsible for checking electrical equipment? Where is this recorded?

Potentially hazardous equipment and materials		
Stage/subject	**Equipment**	**Safe usage**
Foundation stage	Sand, water, play equipment.	Young children will need to be taught to handle equipment safely and to consider how their actions can harm others.
PE	Apparatus use, movement and storage.	In PE lessons, children will need to learn how to use equipment carefully and safely. Equipment should be regularly checked.
Design Technology	Tools or equipment.	As these tools may not be used often, staff will need to talk to children each time about using them carefully.
Science	Living things, pond areas, use of equipment.	Children should be taught to always wash their hands after touching animals and to use any equipment safely.
Food technology	Cooking areas should be regularly checked and care should be taken with cookers.	Cleaning substances should be stored out of reach of small children.
ICT	Computers are in use all the time in schools and should be regularly checked.	Office staff will probably be the only people using them for long periods and should be aware of the importance of taking breaks.
Other electrical items	Equipment used in school will all need to have an annual safety check.	If staff bring their own electrical appliances into school, these should always be checked before use to prevent a risk to others using a portable appliance tester.

Storing and moving equipment

All items should be stored or moved carefully and only by those who are authorised to do so. Adults should not attempt to move items which are heavy or difficult to move. Items which may form a potential hazard should be locked away until they are needed. Storing items safely is important as people will often need to find them quickly and they will need to be able to see where they are and be able to reach them. Staff should ensure that storage areas are kept tidy and materials are not piled up to form a further danger.

▲ Materials should always be stored safely

Accidental breakages or spillages

When breakages and spillages do occur, they will need to be cleaned up as soon as possible to prevent any danger to others. If you are in a situation where an accident has occurred and you are not aware of where to find cleaning equipment, you should not leave the area unattended but send for another member of staff.

Disposal of waste

If you have been carrying out any activities, for example in science, where you need to dispose of waste materials, you should do so in such a way that will not cause harm to others. The school should offer guidance on the disposal of these kinds of materials. If you are in any doubt you should contact your school's health and safety representative.

Ensuring others are aware where you are

You should ensure that the class teacher knows where you are at all times. This is so that in case of emergency, such as fire or a bomb scare, they will be able to find you. Different schools may have different procedures for doing this, so the class teacher should inform you of what to do if you are out of the classroom. It is particularly important if you are taking children away from the classroom for any reason.

External hazards which may be found in school

There may be other hazards which are found outside, for example in playgrounds and pond areas. These will include dangers such as poisonous plants, areas which have not been fenced in and risk of drowning. If you are taking children on a school trip, a member of staff should always visit first to check for potential dangers.

The table below shows some of the hazards which may be found outside the school building.

External hazards	
Type of hazard (outdoor/during school trips)	**What to do**
Playground areas: – broken/faulty equipment – using equipment inappropriately, e.g. skipping ropes, bats and balls	Remove and label **OR** report immediately Warn children or remove
Poisonous plants	Fence off area/warn older children
Litter bins	Keep children away from unsafe bins
Danger from animals	Ensure children always wash their hands after contact. Keep children away from any animal faeces
Pond area	Ensure any cuts on hands are covered before getting wet (risk of leptospirosis – Weil's disease)

Visiting swimming pools

For visits to swimming pools there are set minimum standards in safety. The head teacher is responsible for ensuring that all teaching staff involved have had sufficient training and information to allow them to carry out the sessions safely. There should always be an adult present who is competent in carrying out a rescue and artificial resuscitation. Other helpers will all need to be aware of emergency procedures.

 Case study

You have been asked to accompany Year 5 to their weekly swimming lesson. Although you are aware of emergency procedures, and another teacher will be going to teach the class, the teacher who usually accompanies the group and supervises is off sick and you are unsure whether any other adult in the group is qualified in safety issues.

Speak to your mentor about what you should do in this situation.

Visits to farms

When visiting farms, staff will need to be aware of school guidelines on these visits. The health and safety executive has produced an information sheet – 'Avoiding ill health at open farms – advice to teachers' (AIS23 Supplement). This recommends that schools should ensure that children:

▷ wash their hands thoroughly after contact with animals

▷ cover cuts and grazes on hands with waterproof dressings

▷ eat only in designated areas

▷ stay in areas which are for visitors and keep gates closed

▷ wear appropriate footwear.

Disability Discrimination Act

With the introduction of the Disability Discrimination Act into schools from September 2002, staff need to be increasingly aware of any increase in potential hazards when taking children on school visits. Children should not be excluded from any school visit because of their disability.

Knowledge into action

Ask your mentor if you can investigate an area of your school (indoor or outdoor) for safety. Can you find any potential hazards? What are the school's procedures for reporting these?

School security

Schools need to ensure that they take measures to protect all adults and pupils whilst they are on school premises. This includes making sure that all those who are in school have been signed in and identified. Schools may have different methods for doing this, for example visitors may be issued with badges. If staff notice any unidentified people in the school, they should be challenged immediately. If you are on playground duty and notice anything suspicious, you should also send for help. Schools may also have secure entry and exit points which may make it more difficult for unidentified individuals to enter the premises.

The reasons for increased vigilance in school security follow several well-publicised incidents which have resulted in injury and death within schools, in particular the shootings in Dunblane. The relative ease with which individuals have been able to enter schools and cause harm to children and staff has meant that schools have had to think about how they protect everyone whilst on school premises.

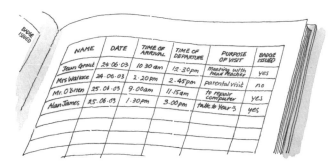

The table in the image shows a signing in book with the following columns and entries:

NAME	DATE	TIME OF ARRIVAL	TIME OF DEPARTURE	PURPOSE OF VISIT	BADGE ISSUED
Jean Grout	24.06.03	10.30 am	12.30 pm	meeting with head teacher	yes
Mrs Wallace	24.06.03	2.20 pm	2.45 pm	parental visit	no
Mr. O'Brien	25.06.03	9.00 am	11.15 am	to repair computer	yes
Alan James	25.06.03	1.30 pm	3.00 pm	talk to Year 3	yes

▲ All schools should have a 'signing in' book for visitors to the school

Keys to good practice
Minimising risks in the learning environment

✔ Be vigilant – always investigate potential dangers.

✔ Use and store equipment safely.

✔ Report anything which is unsafe.

✔ Challenge any unidentified persons – ask your mentor about school policy for what to do in this situation.

Appropriate action to take in an emergency

All workplaces must carry out regular fire practices so that staff are aware of procedures. In a school, this ensures that children also know what to do. These procedures will also apply to bomb scares and any other need for building evacuation.

Your school should have blue fire notices displayed at fire points around the school to indicate what to do in case of fire. If you discover a fire, you should sound the nearest alarm and ensure everyone leaves the building as quickly and calmly as possible. It is important to remain calm and to check that all children and adults have been accounted for. Remember to include any parent helpers or other adults who are in school by checking the school signing-in book.

Knowledge into action

Are regular fire practices carried out in your school? Are there clear guidelines for evacuation and assembly points?

Fire extinguishers

There are different kinds of fire extinguishers, and if you need to use one you should make sure that you read the instructions carefully. These will be printed on the outside of the extinguisher.

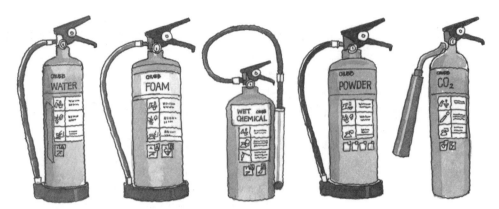

▲ Different types of fire extinguishers

Water – for wood, paper and textiles

Foam – for wood, paper, textiles, petrol, oil, fats, paints etc

Wet chemical – for burning liquid, electrical fires and flammable liquids

Powder – for wood, paper, textiles, petrol, oils, fats, paints, electrical hazards, vehicle protection

CO_2 – for petrol, oils, fats, paints, electrical hazards

Fire blanket – usually kept in a kitchen for smothering a fire or putting around someone whose clothes are on fire.

Evidence collection

Ask your school's health and safety representative if you can accompany him or her on a 'walkround' to check for hazards in the learning environment. This should be a regular occurrence to ensure that staff are vigilant in their day-to-day activities and make sure that the environment is safe for everyone. The kinds of things you are looking for will include:

▶ Scissors or other sharp items left within reach

▶ Items which may easily be tripped over

▶ Electrical items left on, or which have not been safety checked and marked, overloaded plugs

▶ Fire extinguishers which are not regularly checked

▶ Hot drinks around children which could cause injury

▶ Entry and exit points such as gates around the school which are unlocked

▶ Fire doors obstructed

▶ Storage which overhangs on shelves and cupboards

▶ Broken or faulty equipment of any kind

Make sure that you note down any hazards and report them to the premises officer or caretaker at the end of your 'walkround'.

Element 3-10.2 Minimise the risks arising from health emergencies

For this element, you will need to know and understand the following:

▶ minimising risks arising from emergencies
▶ completing accident report forms.

Minimising risks arising from emergencies

What to do in an emergency

There are different kinds of emergencies and conditions that can occur in school. You may find that you are first on the scene in an emergency and need to take action. If you are the only adult in the vicinity, you will need to make sure you follow the correct procedures until help arrives. It is vital to send for help as soon as possible. This should be the ambulance if necessary and the school's qualified first aider.

Different emergencies and what you should do
Injuries – check the injury. For minor injuries such as a bump on the head or a graze, you should apply cold water. If the injury is more serious, you may need to take the victim to the qualified first aider in school. All injuries to the head should be recorded.
Epileptic seizure – do not try to move or restrain the patient. If possible, put something soft beneath their head to prevent them from hurting themselves. Clear a space around them.
Burns and scalds – cool the affected area immediately using cold water. Do not remove any clothes which are stuck to the burn.
Electrocution – cut off the source of electricity by removing the plug. If there is no way to do this, stand on dry insulating material, such as newspaper or a wooden box, and push the victim away from the source using something wooden such as a chair. Do not touch the victim until the electricity has been switched off. After this, place the victim in the recovery position (see page 189).
Choking or difficulty with breathing – if a child, encourage them to cough to dislodge the blockage. Bend the casualty over with the head lower than the chest and slap between the shoulder blades five times using the heel of the hand.
Poisoning – find out what the child has taken or swallowed if possible. Stay with the child and watch for signs of unconsciousness. Take the suspected poison to hospital with you.
Cardiac arrest – if the patient is conscious, place in a half sitting position and support with pillows and cushions. Place another pillow under the knees. Do not give the patient food or water. If the patient becomes unconscious, place in the recovery position (see page 189).

Different emergencies and what you should do (cont.)

Substance abuse – if you can, find out what has happened so that you can inform medical staff. If the person is unconscious, place in the recovery position (see page 189). Do not try to induce vomiting.

Falls – potential and actual fractures: all cases should be treated as actual fractures. Do not attempt to move the casualty. You will need a qualified first aider to come to the scene. Support a fractured leg by tying it to the other leg, using a wide material such as a scarf or tie. If the knee is broken, you must not try to force it straight. If you suspect a fractured arm, support in a sling and secure to the chest. If the arm will not bend, secure by strapping it to the body.

Faints or loss of consciousness – treat those who feel faint by sitting down and putting their head between their knees. If they do faint, lie them on their back and raise their legs to increase blood flow to the brain. Loosen clothing at the neck and keep the patient quiet after regaining consciousness.

Severe bleeding – it is important to reduce the flow of blood as soon as possible. You should summon the first aider and call for help. Lie the casualty down and remove clothing around the wound if possible. Press down hard on it with any absorbent clean material or squeeze the sides together if there is no foreign body in the wound. If possible, raise the wound to above the level of the heart. This will slow the flow of blood. Maintain the pressure for up to ten minutes and then place an absorbent material over the wound and bandage firmly. Do not remove the bandage. If there is a foreign body in the skin, do not remove it but bandage around if possible without putting pressure on the object. If you remove the object, it will cause the victim to lose more blood.

Shock – lie the victim down and treat whatever may be causing the shock. Loosen clothing at the neck to assist breathing. Raise the legs if possible and keep warm. Do not give the victim anything to eat or drink in case they need an anaesthetic, but moisten lips if necessary.

Anaphylactic shock – you may find that there are children in your school who have severe allergies, for example to bee or wasp stings or to food such as nuts, which may cause them to go into anaphylactic shock. You should find out who these children are and what procedures the school has in place in this situation. If you find that a child in your class has an epipen or anapen, you should find out what training is available for their administration. See Unit 3-11 for details on how to administer medicines.

Putting a casualty into the recovery position

If you are dealing with an unconscious person, you will need to place them in the recovery position. This will prevent any blood, vomit or saliva from blocking the windpipe. You should always do this unless you suspect that the victim has a fracture of the spine or neck.

1 Kneel beside the victim and turn their head towards you, lifting it back to open the airway.

2 Place their nearest arm straight down their side and the other arm across their chest. Place the far ankle over the near ankle.

▲ Putting a casualty into the recovery position

3 Whilst holding the head with one hand, hold the victim at the hip by their clothing and turn onto their front by pulling towards you, supporting them with your knees.

4 Lift the chin forward to keep the airway open.

5 Bend the arm and leg nearest to you and pull out the other arm from under the body, palm up.

Potential dangers

If you are treating a patient, you should be aware of the dangers of contamination from blood and other body fluids. Always wear protective gloves if you can when treating an open wound or if you have contact with other body fluids. Many infections such as HIV and hepatitis can be passed on through contact with these fluids.

You should always stay with the casualty and give as much support as you can, both by giving as much care as you are able and by your physical presence. If you feel that you are not able to deal with the situation, you should always do what you can and reassure the patient as much as possible whilst sending for help. Where a child has been injured badly, their parents or carers should be notified immediately. They will need to know exactly what is happening – if the child is being taken to hospital they will need to know where.

Religious and cultural restrictions on the actions which you may be able to take

When dealing with an emergency, you should be aware that signs and symptoms of some illnesses may differ in relation to age and ethnic groups. A young child may show different symptoms of illness from someone who is older. Some religions or cultures may not agree with some treatments – for example, some Muslims may only wash under running water. If you are in any doubts as to what action you can take, always speak to parents first if at all possible.

Knowledge into action

Discuss within your group what you would do in the following situations:

▶ a child has a severe nosebleed whilst you are responsible for a larger group
▶ whilst on playground duty, you notice an unknown individual inside the school boundary which is close to a recreation ground
▶ a child has an epileptic seizure whilst you are working in a class.

Treating others

If others are in the vicinity at the time of the accident, they may need to have support after the initial danger has passed. This could be due to emotional distress or shock, which can have a serious effect. If you are dealing with an emergency situation, you should be aware that taking inappropriate action may be just as dangerous as taking no action if you are not a trained first aider or are not equipped to deal with the emergency. If you have been involved with treating the victim but another person has now taken over, you should offer what support you can to others in the area. This may include giving them privacy and making the area safe.

Completing accident forms

By law, the school will have procedures for recording and reporting accidents. All accidents, whether they are serious or minor, must be recorded. There may be a school accident book and a local authority accident form. The kind of information required will be:

▷ the name of the casualty (child or adult)
▷ what happened
▷ the date and time of the accident
▷ the cause of the accident
▷ the treatment given.

Sunnymead Primary School
Accident report form

Name of casualty . . . .

Exact location of incident . . . .

Date of incident . . . .

What was the injured person doing? . . . .

How did the accident happen? . . . .

What injuries occurred? . . . . ?

Treatment given . . . .

Medical aid sought . . . .

Name of person dealing with incident . . . .

Name of witness . . . .

If casualty was a child, what time were parents informed? . . . .

Was hospital attended? . . . .

Was the accident investigated? . . . . By whom? . . . .

Signed . . . . Position . . . .

▲ An example of an accident report form

Evidence collection

You are working in a Year 3 class in which there are 2 children who have severe nut allergies. They both need to have an epipen, and there is one kept in the school office and one in the classroom. The school gives training in the use of epipens each year which you have attended.

A new parent in the class has brought some biscuits to school as it is her child's birthday, and is giving them out at the end of the school day. She is unaware that the school do not allow this to happen because of the amount of children who have allergies. One of the children with an allergy refuses to take the biscuit, but the other has one and immediately begins to feel unwell. His mother has not yet arrived to collect him. The class teacher calls you over as she knows that you have had training in the use of an epipen and she has not.

▶ Write down what you would do in this situation.

▶ Show how you would give support to the child and ensure that you managed this situation effectively.

End of unit test

1 Why was the Health and Safety at Work etc Act introduced?

2 Name 3 hazards which may be found in a classroom.

3 Why should electrical items brought into school be checked?

4 What kinds of areas may be hazardous outside the school building?

5 What should you do in the event of a burn?

6 How do you put a patient in the recovery position? Practice with a partner.

7 Name 2 ways in which you can help others once expert assistance has arrived to treat a casualty.

8 What are the different kinds of fire extinguisher and their uses?

9 List 4 questions found on an accident form.

10 Why do you need to be careful when handling body fluids?

References

Readers Digest: *What to do in an emergency* (1988)

Tassoni, Penny: *Child care and Education* (Heinemann, 1998)

Websites

www.teachernet.gov.uk/visits (good practice guide to health and safety of pupils on educational visits)

Unit 3-11 Contribute to the health and well-being of pupils

There are three elements to this unit. These are:

3-11.1 Support pupils in adjusting to a new setting
3-11.2 Support pupils in maintaining standards of health and hygiene
3-11.3 Respond to signs of health problems.

This section deals with the care and support given to children whilst adjusting to a new setting. Assistants will need to show that they support the teacher in the kinds of strategies which are used to help and reassure pupils. They will also be able to deal with any particular difficulties which the child is experiencing in settling in. Where pupils have any medical needs, assistants will need to know the school policies for the storage and administration of medicines and how to care for pupils with signs of ill-health (for details of what to do in an emergency, see section 3-10).

Element 3-11.1 Support pupils in adjusting to a new setting

For this element, you will need to know and understand the following:

▶ how to support pupils in adjusting to a new setting
▶ factors which may affect a pupil's ability to adjust to a new setting.

How to support pupils in adjusting to a new setting

If you are helping pupils to adjust to a new setting, this may be for a variety of reasons:

▷ the pupils have just started school in Reception
▷ pupil(s) are joining an existing class
▷ the class is transferring at the start of a new academic year
▷ pupil(s) are re-joining the class after a period of extended absence.

Assistants will need to be able to help pupils in each of these situations to become used to the new setting through a range of strategies. Some children may not need to have much adult intervention to help them to settle in, whilst others may find it more difficult.

▲ Pupils will need help in adjusting to a new classroom

Pupils starting school in Reception

The year group leader (if there is one), class teacher and assistants will all need to discuss the kinds of strategies which they will use with the new group of children. The school may have set guidelines and procedures that are to be used with all children. These may be routine and include:

▷ coming to the school before the start date to meet the class teacher and look at their new classroom

▷ staggering the children's entry so that they start at 5 or 10 minute intervals on the first day

▷ staying for part of the day and building up to include lunchtimes and then afternoons

▷ having separate playtimes from the rest of the school for the first week or two

▷ being shown around the school so that they are aware of different areas and when they are likely to use them (office, hall/dining hall, playground etc).

As the children become settled in school, they will gradually learn the rules and routines which they will be expected to follow. This process will take place over time as the children become used to being in a school environment.

Knowledge into action

Find out about the procedures that teachers in the Reception classes in your school follow for settling in new children. Do they have any that are different from those listed above?

Pupil(s) joining an existing class

When new pupils join an already established class, they may find it quite difficult to come into a class where the majority of children already know the rules and routines. Assistants and teachers will need to work together to help them to adjust and feel part of the class. The kinds of strategies that could be used in this situation would include:

▷ encouraging other children to make new arrivals feel welcome through interacting with them and showing them around

▷ showing them around the classroom and class routines

▷ giving them information about the school that you feel would be useful for them to know – playtimes, lunchtimes, location of key areas, class rules.

▷ being approachable if the child needs help in any way.

▲ When new pupils join a class they need to know the class rules

Case study

John has come into a Year 4 class from another school. You are an assistant in the class and notice that he is quite quiet and is finding it difficult to talk to other children.

Can you provide a list of strategies like the ones above, for example giving him a 'buddy' or partnering him with different children and outline some of the pros or cons.

Class is transferring at the start of a new academic year

If you support an individual child, you may be in a position where you are moving with all the children into a different class. This may make the process easier for them, since they will have an adult they recognise who will know them. However, children will become more used to changing class each year as they progress up the school and most will be excited to be moving up into the next year group. If you are a teaching assistant working within a class you can help the children to settle in by:

▷ emphasising the importance of moving into the next year group
▷ showing them the layout of the classroom

▲ Children in a different year group may have new responsibilities

- encouraging them to join in with class activities
- discussing with them any rules or responsibilities which are specific to the year group, for example 'Now you are in Year 6, you are allowed to go in first at lunchtime', 'Years 3 and 4 are in charge of changing the words on the overhead projector in assembly'
- being approachable and available for any questions the children may have

Pupil(s) are rejoining the class after a period of extended absence

Sometimes pupils may leave the class for a period, for example if they are travellers or if they have special needs and have required help within another setting for a time. They may find it difficult to adjust to a new environment or be self-conscious about returning and their reasons for being away from the school. You can help them to settle back into the class by:

- being available for them to talk through any concerns
- supporting their integration with other children
- helping them with any specific problems.

 Case study

Paul is from a travelling family and often misses school for extended periods. He is not unhappy about returning to the school environment but often finds it difficult to settle and focus on his work. Discuss in your group how you could encourage Paul to become used to the school and become involved with other children.

Factors which may affect a pupil's ability to adjust to a new setting

Sometimes, pupils may find it difficult to settle due to outside factors which make it more difficult for them than for other children. The kinds of factors this may include are:

- the home background of the child – the child may have a disruptive or traumatic home life
- the care history – the pupil may not like change if there have been changes in carer at home
- if the child speaks English or Welsh as an additional language
- any special educational needs which the child has – this may affect the child's understanding of what is happening.

You will need to be able to support children in all these situations through discussions with teachers, parents and helpers. These children may need more reassurance and help and may sometimes display challenging behaviour (see also Unit 3-1 page 161 for strategies for managing this).

It is vital that the class teacher is aware of any problems or difficulties that a child has in adjusting or settling in. If you notice or find out about any issues or if a parent or other member of staff tells you about a child's home circumstances and you do not think the teacher is aware, you must talk to the teacher about it immediately.

If the child speaks English or Welsh as an additional language, there may be a variety of factors which make it difficult to settle in a new setting. As each child will be different owing to circumstances and experiences, these will vary from case to case.

 ## Knowledge into action

Speak to other staff in your school about procedures the school uses for helping children to adjust if they are in a new environment.

 ## Evidence collection

Either at the beginning of a new term with your class or when a new child comes into your school, ask if you can work in that class and observe and help the child to settle at various times over the next few weeks.

Keep a log of the child's progress and note down any strategies that you use to help the child to settle and feel part of the school. Also show how you encourage other pupils to interact with him or her.

If there are any problems, record how you dealt with them and reported them to the teacher.

Element 3-11.2 Support pupils in maintaining standards of health and hygiene

For this element, you will need to know and understand the following:

▶ school policies and practices relating to health and hygiene issues
▶ school policies and practices relating to medical issues.

School policies relating to health and hygiene issues

The school should have policies relating to the way in which health issues are managed in school. These will include routines and procedures for everyday health and hygiene such as washing hands before lunch and after using the toilet. All staff should be aware of how children need to be reminded about health issues and how these will affect themselves and others. The school should have a policy for PSHEC (Personal, social and health education and citizenship) which will include information about the way in which children are taught about health. This may be through cross-curricular activities or taught on its own. Pupils will need to learn about healthy lifestyles and may have visits from the community such as the school nurse, ambulance service and road safety officer.

If you need to answer any questions from pupils about health and hygiene, you should make sure that you are following school policy.

Case study

Amira is a classroom assistant in a Year 1 class. The children have been incubating eggs as part of their topic on living things. Once they have hatched, Amira has been allowing the children to handle the chicks when they are a few days old. However, Amira forgets to remind the children to wash their hands after handling the chicks.

1 Do you think that this is important?

2 What might be the repercussions?

You may notice that pupils have different attitudes from home towards health and hygiene issues. Some families may bring their children up in more clean and hygienic environments than others and this may be reflected in the child's clothing or personal hygiene. Different factors may affect a child's personal hygiene requirements:

▷ Age – very young children may not yet have established routines for cleanliness and hygiene.

▷ Gender – boys and girls may have different attitudes towards keeping clean.

▷ Cultural/racial background – this may affect the importance of cleanliness, particularly if the child has a religion which requires them to be extremely clean.

▷ Specific medical conditions – children may need specific help, for example if they are catheterised or need to wear nappies.

These factors may also affect the actions you can take when attending to a child's signs of ill-health. For example, if a child already has a medical condition and is on medication you will need to inform any others who come to attend to them.

You will also need to adhere to health and safety regulations and guidelines when you are attending to children's health. Guidance on health and safety regulations will be given in the school's health and safety and child protection policies and through information provided by the local authority. The main points to remember are:

▷ If children need to be changed or undressed following wetting or soiling themselves they should do this themselves if possible and in private. Parents may need to be called if this is not possible. If staff need to change children for any reason they should not do it on their own but should have another member of staff present.

▷ Where a child's necessary medication needs to be administered other than orally, for example through a suppository, staff should again always be accompanied by another member of staff.

▷ Ask for assistance in any situation in which you feel uncomfortable about administering medication or healthcare unaccompanied by another adult.

▷ Always report any possible signs of abuse which you may notice when administering medical or health care. (see also Unit 3-1 page 156)

▷ You will need to make sure you follow the school's guidelines for informing parents about hygiene issues. It is important that you are sensitive if you are asked to speak to a parent where there has been an issue concerning hygiene.

School policies and practices relating to medical issues

The school may have a number of policies relating to the medical care of pupils whilst they are in the setting. These may follow guidelines set out by the local education authority which should be available to all schools. You should know where to go to ask about them and to find out about your responsibilities.

When the child first enters school, parents will be asked to provide details about their health which may include whether their child has any allergies, medication and so on.

These kinds of records will be kept in the child's file, although if there is any medication which needs to be administered in school or medical treatment for conditions such as asthma or allergies, these should be kept in a central area such as the school office and treated as confidential. There may be a member of staff who is responsible for administering medication although this is a voluntary role and should

St Marks Primary School
Declaration of Health Form

Child's surname . . . . Date of birth . . . .

First names . . . .

Address . . . .

. . . .

Telephone number (home) . . . .

Parent/carer's work/mobile telephone numbers:

Mother . . . . Father . . . .

Name and address of GP . . . .

. . . . Telephone no . . . .

Health Details

Does your child have:

Asthma YES/NO   Eczema YES/NO   Epilepsy YES/NO   Diabetes YES/NO

Any allergies . . . .

Details of medication . . . .

Is there any other information you feel we should know about your child?

. . . .

. . . .

▲ An example of a Declaration of Health Form

not be expected of staff. If there is not a member of staff who is prepared to administer medicines, parents should be informed in writing and told that an ambulance will be called immediately in the event of an emergency.

 Find out about...

Whether there is a volunteer in your school who administers medication to children and how often they are called upon to do it. What training have they had?

Medical conditions which may require medication to be administered in schools may include:

▷ **Asthma:** children needing inhalers due to a respiratory condition should have access to these quickly in case of emergency.

▲ Different types of inhalers

▷ **Diabetes:** if hypoglycaemia occurs the child will need to take oral glucose, for example food, glucose tablets or glucose gel.

▷ **Epilepsy:** children who are on medication for epilepsy are seldom required to take it during school hours as it is usually taken twice a day. However, if medication is required three times a day, volunteers in the staff may be asked to administer it.

▷ **Anaphylactic shock:** some children have severe allergic reactions to certain substances such as nuts or milk and can suffer anaphylactic shock. The only way

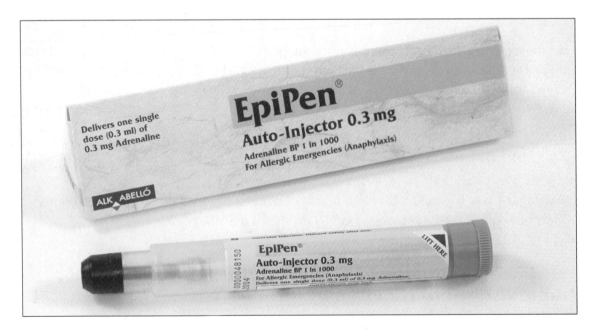

▲ An example of an EpiPen

this can be treated in school is through the administration of adrenaline via an EpiPen or AnaPen. For this to be administered, staff will need to have had specific training.

▷ **Attention Deficit Hyperactivity Disorder (ADHD):** school aged children are being increasingly diagnosed with this disorder and the most common form of medication which is used to treat these children is Ritalin.

Schools may also be asked to administer antibiotics and may have a policy as to whether or not they do this. If antibiotics are prescribed to be taken three times a day it is not necessary to administer them during school time, but children who need four doses may need to have one at lunchtime. It is likely that the school will have a policy as to whether or not they will administer medication which has not been prescribed by a doctor. They should also keep a record of medication given. Medication that is to be administered in school should always be correctly labelled and locked in a safe place until required.

Administration of medicines record sheet					
Name of pupil					
Date	Time	Name of medication	Dose given	Any reactions	Signature

▲ A record of medication given must be kept

Keys to good practice
Administering medicines in school

✔ Gain parental consent to administer medication and keep signature.

✔ Keep a record of medication given as shown above.

✔ Store all medication in a safe place and keep labelled.

✔ Keep any urgent medication close to the child.

✔ Keep a list of children who have medication in school.

✔ Make sure medicines are not out of date.

Access to routine and emergency medical care

In school there must be at least one qualified first aider who is trained to administer immediate help to casualties with common injuries or illnesses whilst in school. (see also Unit 2-1 page 14) They will be trained to deal with routine medical incidents such as bumps on the head and cuts and grazes. You should be aware of who these people are so that you are able to send for them in an emergency along with the emergency services. Where children have needed medical treatment or have hurt themselves, the school may decide to telephone the parent to tell them what has happened. Any injuries to the head should also be recorded. Staff will need to be aware of the school's confidentiality requirements when recording and reporting health problems.

Find out about...

Where your school keeps records of injuries and bumps to the head. Are parents usually called when this happens?

The school may have to decide whether to phone a parent if the child is ill or has been hurt. If the child is very ill, distressed or badly injured, the parent will need to be informed immediately by telephone. You will need to give reassurance and support to children who are ill or suffering from a condition which is distressing to them. The support or advice which you give them will be dependent on the age and stage of development of the child.

Case study

Michael is in Reception and has conjunctivitis. The school policy states that he should be sent home as the condition is highly contagious. Michael has become very distressed about his eyes and says that they itch and hurt. He is worried because he has come out of his classroom and the school have called his mother.

1 What would you say to Michael to reassure him?

2 How would the treatment and advice be different with an older child?

Evidence collection

Ask your class teacher if you can work with 2 or 3 children to do a small project or presentation on basic health and hygiene. Include:-

▶ basic hygiene skills – why is it important?

▶ school routines for health and hygiene (for example, washing hands before lunch, going to first aid when necessary)

▶ how we can help others who may have health or medical needs in school?

If your children do a presentation, ask if you can tape or video it to use as evidence.

Element 3-11.3 Respond to signs of health problems

For this element, you will need to know and understand the following:

▶ signs and symptoms of some common illnesses

▶ maintaining your own health and safety when dealing with pupils who have health problems.

Signs and symptoms of some common illnesses

All staff should be aware of the kinds of illnesses that may occur in children. They should also be alert to physical signs that may show they are incubating an illness. This can vary between illnesses, from 1 day to 3 weeks in some cases. General signs that children are 'off colour' may include:

▷ pale skin

▷ flushed cheeks

▷ different (quiet, clingy, irritable) behaviour

▷ rings around the eyes

The Department of Health has issued a useful poster to schools which could be displayed in the first aid area as a quick reference: 'Guidance on infection control in schools and nurseries'. This clearly sets out some common illnesses and their characteristics. Some of these are listed below although this list is not exhaustive.

Common illnesses and their characteristics

Illness and symptoms	Recommended time to keep off school/ treatment	Comments
Chickenpox – patches of red spots with white centres (itchy).	For five days from onset of rash. Treat with calomine lotion to relieve itching.	Not necessary to keep at home until scars heal.
German measles (rubella) – pink rash on head, trunk and limbs. Slight fever, sore throat.	For five days from onset of rash. Treat by resting.	Child is most infectious before diagnosis is made. Keep away from pregnant women.
Impetigo – small red pimples on the skin which break down and weep.	Until legions are crusted and healed. Treat with antibiotic cream or medicine.	Antibiotic treatment may speed up healing. Wash hands well after touching the child's skin.
Ringworm – contagious fungal infection of the skin, shows as circular flaky patches.	None. Treat with anti-fungal ointment, may require antibiotics.	Needs treatment by GP.
Diarrhoea and vomiting	Until diarrhoea and vomiting has settled and for 24 hours after. No specific diagnosis or treatment, although keep giving clear fluids (no milk).	
Conjunctivitis – inflammation or irritation of the membranes lining the eyelids.	Wash with warm water on cotton wool swab. GP may prescribe cream.	None (although schools may have different policies on this).
Measles – fever, runny eyes, sore throat and cough. Red rash, often starting from the head and spreading downwards.	Rest, plenty of fluids, paracetamol for fever.	Now more likely with some parents refusing MMR innoculation.
Meningitis – fever, headache, stiff neck and blotchy skin. Dislike of light. Symptoms may develop very quickly.	Urgent medical attention, antibiotics.	Can have severe complications and be fatal.
Tonsilitis – inflammation of tonsils by infection. Very sore throat, fever, earache, enlarged red tonsils which may have white spots.	Treat with antibiotics, rest.	Can also cause ear infections.

Staff will need to be alert to signs and symptoms of these kinds of illnesses and notice changes in children's behaviour which may indicate that they are unwell. Children often develop symptoms more quickly than adults as they may have less resistance to infection. You should also be careful if the child has a medical or cultural condition which means that he or she should not have a particular kind of treatment or medication. These kinds of issues should always be clearly marked on the child's records, whether they are written or computerised.

Maintaining your own health and safety when dealing with pupils who have health problems

You must remember to think about your own safety when you are dealing with pupils who have health and medical problems. You should make sure that you are aware of the kinds of situations which are potentially hazardous when dealing with first aid situations. Remember good personal hygiene at all times and that the risk of transmission of infection is minimal if staff adopt sensible precautions:

▷ cuts to the hands should be covered by a waterproof dressing to minimise risk of infection

▷ always wear disposable gloves when dealing with blood and body fluids

▷ wash your hands after removing the gloves and prior to eating or drinking

▷ any spillages of blood or body fluids must be reported to the caretaker immediately.

Other medical professionals who come into school or ask for information about children may include the school nurse or visitors from medical establishments who

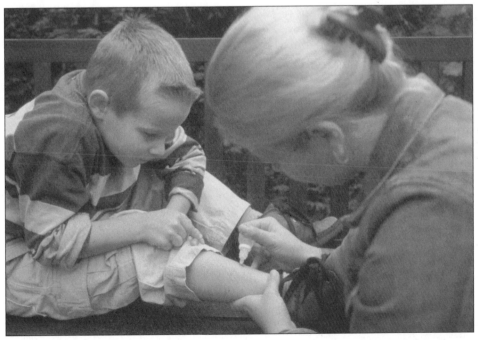

▲ You must remember to think about your own safety when dealing with pupils who have health problems

come to discuss children who have special needs. If children have any medical condition which you feel needs to be discussed with another professional, you should speak to the class teacher or SENCO.

Sometimes, the child may be in a class where there are cases of head-lice, ringworm and other conditions which are contagious. The school will in these circumstances usually write to inform parents if there are more than one or two cases in one class. When keeping children off school, parents should be aware of the school's normal policies for different illnesses. For example, if a child has had sickness or diarrhoea, the school may say they must have been better for 24 hours before coming back.

Contacting parents

The school may have to decide whether to phone a parent if the child is ill or has been hurt. If the child is very ill, distressed or badly injured, the parent will need to be informed immediately by telephone. (See Unit 3-10 page 189 for informing parents in cases of emergency)

Holy Cross Infant School

Dear Parent

We have been informed by a parent that one of the children in your child's class has had to be treated for head lice. We feel it is important to inform you so that you will be extra vigilant and take the simple steps needed to combat the problem.

In a normal school environment, where children work and play closely together, head lice find it easy to transfer from head to head. Remember, head lice prefer clean hair, so the possibility of infection is quite high. Your child has as much chance of being infected as any other.

Fortunately head lice are easy to treat and you should follow the attached guidelines from the health authority to do this.

As a preventative, the only form of treatment is to comb your child's hair thoroughly every day and if your child has long hair, to keep it tied back.

Yours sincerely,

J A Sampson

Headteacher

▲ Sample of a standard letter for head lice

Evidence collection

This is a simulated evidence activity as you may not have the opportunity to act in a health emergency but you will need to know what to do.

You are a teaching assistant in a class of Year 5 children. Ben, in your class has a nut allergy and an EpiPen both in the classroom and school office. At playtime, his friend tells you that Ben has had a biscuit which may contain nuts and that he is starting to feel unwell. You have had training in the use of an EpiPen.

▶ Discuss in your groups in detail what you would do in this situation and how you would go about helping Ben.

▶ Show how you would comply with school policy and procedures for recording the incident.

End of unit test

1 Name 2 circumstances in which you may need to help pupils adjust to a new setting.

2 Give an example of how schools might help children in Reception classes to settle in.

3 Name 3 of the more common medical conditions that may require medication to be administered in school.

4 How might the school find out whether children need any specific medical attention?

5 What kinds of precautions should you take when dealing with pupils who have hygiene, health and medical needs?

6 When would staff need to report or record any medical treatment?

7 What might influence a pupil's attitude to personal hygiene?

8 In what kinds of situations would you require another adult to be present?

9 Name 5 common illnesses that may be found in schools.

10 What professionals may come to the school to discuss with children or give information about health issues?

References

Stanway, Penny: *Mothercare Guide to Child Health* (Conran Octopus 1988)

Useful Addresses

British Epilepsy Association – New Anstey House, Gate Way Drive, Yeadon, Leeds LS19 7NW (0113 439393)

British Diabetic Association – 10 Parkway, London NW1 7AA (0207 323 1531)

Asthma Society – 300 Upper Street, London N1 2XX (0207 226 2260)

Department of Health: www.doh.gov.uk

Websites

www.phls.co.uk – information on infectious diseases

www.wiredforhealth.gov.uk – further information

Unit 3-17 Support the use of information and communication technology in the classroom

There are two elements to this unit. These are:

3-17.1 Prepare ICT equpment for use in the classroom
3-17.2 Support classroom use of ICT equipment.

ICT plays a major role in the school curriculum as it can be a part of all subject areas. There is now a statutory requirement for the application of ICT in the core subjects (English, Maths and Science) at Key Stage 1 and in all subjects except PE at Key Stage 2. In the Foundation Stage, children will begin to learn to use ICT equipment in the classroom and learn appropriate vocabulary. This means that you will need to be able to support children when using a range of ICT equipment in school. For a fuller definition of the use of ICT across the curriculum, see page 39 of the National Curriculum handbook for England or www.nc.uk.net.

This unit is about ensuring that ICT equipment is available and ready to use when required and that you know how to support teachers and pupils when preparing and using equipment safely. You should also know what to do if you find any faults with equipment and know who is responsible for maintenance so that you are able to report these straight away.

Element 3-17.1 Prepare ICT equipment for use in the classroom

For this element, you will need to know and understand the following:

▶ the types of ICT equipment you will need to use in the classroom
▶ how to prepare equipment for use
▶ reporting equipment faults.

The types of ICT equipment you will need to use in the classroom

When working as an assistant in a primary classroom, you will be expected to know how to prepare and use different ICT equipment. This may range from setting up computers in classrooms and computer suites to knowing how to operate recording equipment. You should make sure that you are familiar with the kinds of equipment you will need to use. These may include:

▷ **Classroom computers and related equipment such as printers** There are many different computers and printers available and you will need to know how to operate the systems used in the school. Computers may usually be kept in classrooms although some schools also have computer suites or rooms.

▷ **Interactive whiteboards** These are increasingly being used in schools and you will need to be shown how to use them. They will usually be connected to a main computer and are a useful demonstration tool when working with groups of children.

▷ **Recording and playback equipment** Most classrooms will have access to tape recorders, CD's and videos. You will need to know where these can be found, how to find extension leads and where to find keys to unlock storage cupboards if necessary.

▷ **Overhead projectors and screens** These will almost certainly be stored away until needed as it is unlikely that they will be permanently kept in classrooms. You will need to find out where they are kept so that you can get them out for use in the learning environment. You may need to ask caretakers or technicians to get them out for you to use.

▷ **Roamers, pixies and other directional equipment** These will also be stored away until they need to be used. You will need some training before you use them as you will need to be clear exactly what you are doing when working with the children. They may also have batteries that will sometimes need to be charged up before use.

▲ You will be expected to use a variety of ICT equipment

Case study

Carol is working as an assistant in an infant school. She has only been at the school for a few weeks when there is a wet playtime and she is asked to set up some video equipment in the hall. Carol assumes it will be an ordinary television and video but when she gets there she finds that it is a projector which she has not been shown how to use.

1 What would you do in Carol's position?

2 What could be done to avoid this from happening?

Knowledge into action

Ask if you can meet your school's ICT co-ordinator. Find out about the kinds of resources your school has for ICT and what you might be required to set up or use. Ask whether you can have training if necessary.

How to prepare equipment for use in the classroom

When you are preparing equipment for use, you will need to make sure that you are clear about exactly what you need to do. If necessary, you may need to have training in how to operate different items of equipment. You may also need to find out how particular computer programmes work. It is a good idea to try out the programme yourself, even if the class teacher has already given you instructions.

Location and use of equipment

You should know what ICT equipment is available in the school and where it is kept so that you will be able to find it when needed. You may need to book equipment for use, or it may be timetabled if different classes need to use it. Different systems may mean that schools check equipment in and out and need to record where it is in case it is not replaced after use. Consumables such as spare paper, bulbs or printer ink should be stored so that they are safe but accessible when needed.

Knowledge into action

Find out what system your school has for the use of ICT equipment. Do you need to record when you use and replace it?

Following manufacturers' instructions

It is important to ensure that instruction booklets for individual items of equipment are easily accessible. Staff need to be able to make sure that equipment is being set up and used correctly, and it is useful to be able to use a troubleshooting section if there are any problems. You will therefore need to know where any instruction manuals are kept.

Computers and peripheral equipment

If you have been asked to prepare computers for use, you will need to find out whether you need to book or timetable them for use by your class. Your school may have procedures for this and you may need to find out about these from the class teacher or ICT subject manager. You will also need to make sure that you know how to set up any computers which are used within your own classroom, and are able to access any CD-ROMS or printers which are needed. If you need to use computer suites with or without the class teacher, you will need to know how to access equipment and the use of any passwords. Always make sure that there are no safety issues which need to be addressed, for example the length of time a child should spend looking at a screen. You will need also to know which computers have modems and internet access in case this is needed.

Interactive whiteboards

You will need to find out where interactive whiteboards are in the school and learn how to use these if you are expected to be able to do so.

Knowledge into action

How confident are you when working with computers? Are you able to work with simple programs and access the internet? If you are not confident with computers you may need to speak to your supervisor or mentor about your training needs.

Recording and playback equipment

You will need to make sure you have access to this equipment when it is required and know how to use it. You may need to prepare recording equipment such as videos for

▲ Children need to be given opportunities to develop their ICT skills in the classroom

use in the classroom, which may involve booking or unlocking from storage and finding the correct place on the tape. If children are using items such as tape recorders, they should be taught how to use them from an early age. It is important that they learn how to operate the tape recorders, by switching on and off and learning vocabulary such as eject, rewind, record, and so on. This will involve teaching groups of children so that they can show others and will develop their self-help skills. It is important that very young children should be given guidance when they first start to use this equipment as it is easily damaged by incorrect use.

Overhead projectors and screens

You may be asked to prepare overhead projectors for use in the classroom or other areas in the school such as the hall or staff room. This will involve removing the equipment from wherever it is stored and setting it up so that it is ready for use. You will need to ensure that there are no safety issues such as trailing cables around the projector.

Roamers, floor turtles, pixies and other directional equipment

These are used for developing concepts such as programming and directional skills. They will need to be kept in a centralised area in school and may be time-tabled for use by different classes. You will need to know how they work and make sure that you have a suitable area in which to use them. This may be an indoor or outdoor area.

Case study

Lauren has been sent to the computer suite with a group of 10 children to work on some data handling activities. Although she has set up the computers before the session started, some of them are no longer logged on and she is unable to access the programme that the group needs to use.

1 What should Lauren do in this situation?

2 If she is still unable to access the programme, what should her next steps be?

Keys to good practice
Preparing equipment

✔ Check availability of equipment and accessories before use.

✔ Ensure that you know how to use all required equipment and have all the information needed.

✔ Check that you have switched on and the equipment is ready to use.

✔ Ensure you know the location of any consumables, for example printer ink, batteries.

✔ Make sure any faults, difficulties or safety issues are reported to the teacher and maintenance officer.

Reporting equipment faults

Electrical equipment which is used in school should always at least have an annual safety check, but if you find any faults in the equipment whilst preparing or using it this should always be reported, however minor. The school should have procedures to follow, such as writing in a maintenance book, but you should also inform the teacher and whoever is responsible for repair or maintenance. This may sometimes be the school's ICT co-ordinator, but increasingly schools will have technicians who will monitor and repair ICT equipment as it is a very time-consuming role. Faulty equipment should then be labelled and isolated from any power source.

If you are setting up equipment and you find a problem, it may be helpful to go through a checklist to see if you can fix the problem yourself.

Equipment faults – checklist

▷ Make sure equipment is turned on properly. In cases of roamers and pixies, ensure that batteries are charged.

▷ Ensure you have turned on all items of equipment – sometimes printers, monitors or scanners may be plugged in and switched on separately.

▷ Ensure plugs are not overloaded.

▷ Only use the correct accessories with each item of equipment.

▷ If there are instruction or troubleshooting manuals available, see whether you can resolve the problem yourself using these.

If you have problems when using ICT equipment or computer programs, you may need to leave what you are doing and report the problem. This is because if you are working with individuals or groups of children it is unlikely that you will be able to sort it out and manage the children at the same time.

 Evidence collection

In your evidence collection for this element, you may need to use simulation in order to obtain evidence in relation to reporting equipment faults and making faulty equipment safe and secure.

Harriet is working in a Year 4 class and has to prepare some roamers for use later in the day. She has had some difficulty in locating the equipment and because of this she has less time to get it ready for use. Harriet has not used the roamers before and does not have time to read the instruction manual or safety instructions. She has a rough idea how to use them and feels that this is sufficient.

▶ Write down what you think Harriet should have done if she was limited in the time available to get the equipment ready.

▶ What should Harriet do if she is unable to operate the equipment or if she discovers a fault?

▶ Should Harriet allow children to use the roamers on this occasion?

Element 3-17.2 Support classroom use of ICT equipment

For this element, you will need to know and understand the following:

▶ school policy and the relevant legislation for the use of computers

▶ how to support the development of ICT skills in pupils.

School policy and relevant legislation for the use of computers

School policy relating to the use of ICT

The school should have an ICT policy which will give guidelines for using and working with ICT in the classroom. There may be a variety of issues to be considered when using ICT equipment. These may be set routines and guidance for the use of equipment

---

Perry Vale School ICT Policy

ICT is changing the lives of everyone. Through teaching ICT, we equip children to participate in a rapidly changing world where work and leisure activities are increasingly transformed by technology. It enables us to find, explore, analyse, exchange and present information. At Perry Vale School, we focus on developing the skills necessary for children to be able to use information in a discriminating and effective way. ICT skills are a major factor in enabling children to be confident, creative and independent learners.

The aims of ICT are to help children:

▶ to develop their capability in finding, selecting and using information

▶ to use ICT for effective and appropriate communication

▶ to monitor and control events, both real and imaginary

▶ to apply hardware and software to creative and appropriate uses of information

▶ to apply ICT to develop their language and maths skills.

As the aims of ICT are to equip children with the skills necessary to use technology to become independent learners, the teaching style that we adopt is as active and practical as possible. ICT is taught as a discrete subject in which we give children direct instruction on how to use hardware or software. These skills then support individuals or groups of children in their use of computers to help them in whatever they are trying to study. So, for example, children might use a computer-based program to investigate a science topic or an internet-based program to practice their numeracy skills.

▲ An example of part of an ICT policy

---

which all individuals should use, for example children to sign a checklist to say when they have used equipment.

The school policy should state the aims and objectives of the school with regard to the children's experiences and opportunities in ICT. There will also be requirements for safety and for storage and security of ICT equipment.

There may be a borough or school policy on use of the Internet and the availability of websites which are suitable for schools. Some schools may have their own websites, which will raise issues with photos of children as parents may not wish their children's photo to be available on the Internet. It may be that your school routinely asks parents for this information but if you know that photographs are to be used, this should be checked.

Knowledge into action

Find out about the measures your school has in place for preventing the spread of viruses through the school computers.

Legislation and regulations relating to the use of ICT

Several legal requirements exist which are relevant to the use of ICT in schools. Assistants should be aware of these and make sure that any information which is confidentially held or seen is not passed on to others. If you have access to school computers

---

Relevant legislation for the use of ICT in schools

Data Protection Act 1998 This has implications for the use of data which is held on school computers and how it is used. Individuals have the right to know what information is held and any information about the children in the school should only be used by the school and not passed on to a third party. Any data which the school holds should be protected against unauthorised access by appropriate security measures.

Child Protection The 1989 Children Act outlines a set of principles which everyone should follow when children are involved. These are to ensure that the welfare of the child will always come first. The local authority may have guidelines for child protection and how information is kept on computers. Staff should ensure that any information which is held about children is kept confidential within the school and any work or results which are published do not contain children's names or other personal information.

Copyright If the school has CD-ROMs and other software, these must only be used by the school and not by other parties and multiple copies of programmes should not be made.

Software licensing This is important in the case of schools as they should be aware of which licences they should have with regard to software held in school. There are different kinds of licence depending on the intended use of the software, for example single use or across a network.

---

containing information about children for example, it is important that you only use them as they are intended and do not leave computer screens on for others to read.

Guidelines for keeping information secure:

▷ Computer systems should not be left unattended when personal information is accessible.

▷ Passwords should keep information secure.

▷ Passwords should not be displayed in office or classroom areas.

▷ Disks and files should be locked away when not in use.

▷ Always review and dispose of any unwanted personal data.

How to support the development of ICT skills in pupils

When you are supporting pupils in the use of ICT, you should have an awareness of the kinds of skills which are being developed in pupils of different ages. There should be a clear progression from the expectations of the Foundation Stage through to children at the top of the Primary phase at Year 6.

Knowledge into action

Find out if you can observe ICT in different age groups within your school. What kinds of skills are children learning to use independently in the Foundation stage? How will these skills help them when they are further up the school?

Staff will need to understand and follow the Foundation Stage and National Curriculum for ICT when working with pupils. The class teacher will have long, medium and short term plans (see page 58) which will highlight the skills to be taught in ICT and in which areas pupils will need to be supported. You should be able to support pupils whilst developing their confidence and independence when using ICT equipment. You will be able to do this by developing skills such as:

Basic user skills Sometimes it is tempting to intervene when pupils are using computers and other equipment, especially if they are just starting to learn how to use them. You should try to ensure that you guide them whilst allowing them to operate equipment independently. You can do this by guiding them through the task verbally or by showing them first and then asking them to repeat what you have done. The kinds of basic skills you may be helping children to develop will be:

▷ using a mouse or keyboard

▷ switching on and closing down equipment and following on screen instructions

▷ using different software packages such as word processing, spreadsheets, databases and graphics.

Stage of learning	ICT skills
Foundation Stage	ICT comes under the Foundation Stage area of 'Knowledge and Understanding of the World'. Children will start to become aware of technology in the home and school environments. They will start to use ICT equipment such as computers and programmable toys and develop their language to use related vocabulary. Children at this stage will be using simple programmes on computers which are designed to help them to develop their mouse and basic keyboard skills. For very young children, smaller mice and simplified keyboards are available through ICT and special educational needs catalogues
Key Stage 1	Children at this stage will need to develop their Knowledge, Skills and Understanding through working with a range of ICT skills and tools. They will need to learn how to access, enter and save as well as retrieve information. Pupils will also start to plan and give instructions, and use a variety of forms to present information. Finally, they should be taught to evaluate their work to help them to develop their ideas and describe the effects of their actions.
Key Stage 2	At this stage, children will use ICT to support work in other subjects. They will need to find, prepare and interpret information using ICT, be aware of their audience and review what they have done. To do this, they will need to be able to use a variety of software and the Internet and interpret information as to its accuracy.

Children may be working at different levels in ICT as with other subjects and the class teacher may ask you to help children with different programmes depending on their ability.

 Think about it

Observe your class teacher when working with a group of children, **either** in a computer suite **or** within the classroom. How do they manage the children to ensure that they are all occupied on a task which is matched to their ability? Find out how your class teacher assesses ICT skills.

Selecting and using appropriate software packages The class teacher should give guidance when selecting software for use in the classroom as it will usually be related to other work which the children are doing. For example, if using the computer during the Literacy Hour, you may be supporting children who are working on a spelling programme. For work on mathematical programmes, the children may be using databases or spreadsheets. It is important that you use appropriate software for the age range in which you are working. You will need to use their own existing knowledge as a starting point when helping them to use appropriate software for the task. Care should be taken when selecting software packages and schools should be able to look at these on approval. This is because although many will state the age range they are aimed at, this may still be unsuitable for use within a class owing to the intervention necessary.

Accessing and using learning programmes You will need to be able to use a computer programme which you have been asked to without needing assistance as this will interrupt both the teacher and the pupil you are supporting. Most programmes will be straightforward if aimed at the primary age range, but you should have had sight of them before you start. Some of these will be CD-ROMs and programmes which are already on the school's computer, but there will also be a selection of primary age materials through the Internet, which are easy to access (see websites at end of unit). The programme selected should be straightforward for the children to use and not too time-consuming or too short for realistic use in the classroom. Some programmes are unsuitable as they take too long to complete, or require adult input to restart at frequent intervals.

Children may need support when accessing learning programmes from CD-ROMs and computer discs and you should do this by talking them through each stage if they are unsure. Older children may need to write themselves reminders for accessing programmes. You may also need to demonstrate to children how to use tapes and videos and how to find the correct place using the counters on machines.

 Case study

Janet has been asked to work with pairs of Year 1 children on the class computer. The programme she is using requires the children to spell groups of words within a certain time limit. Although the programme is useful, after every 5 minutes Janet needs to reset the computer to the beginning of the programmme as it is too complicated for the children to do themselves. Without an assistant, the class teacher is unable to use this programme.

Accessing information Children will need to learn how to access information from computer files, CD-ROMs and the Internet. You will need to help them to gradually build up these skills as they use computers to help them in their work in other subjects.

Using electronic communication systems Pupils will begin to use the Internet and email towards the end of Key Stage One and throughout Key Stage Two. They should be encouraged to use their research skills through finding out specific information, for example 'What can you find out about whales?' This will give them a focus and help them to interpret the information in their own way. You can support them by showing them steps which they should work through to reach the information they need.

If you are using the Internet and email, your school computers will be at risk from viruses and this will need to be controlled within school. Your school's ICT co-ordinator should be able to tell you what steps your school is taking to prevent this.

Safety when using ICT equipment

When using all these methods to develop ICT skills in pupils, assistants should also be aware of the risks associated with using equipment and how these can be minimised. Equipment should be safe to use as long as it is used properly and checked regularly. Children should always be taught to shut down computers correctly after use as they can be damaged if turned off incorrectly.

Keys to good practice
Using ICT equipment

✔ Check the equipment regularly and report any faults.

✔ Use only the correct accessories with each item of equipment.

✔ Ensure that the equipment is being used safely and intervene when it is not.

✔ Store equipment safely when not in use.

Evidence collection

In your evidence collection for this element, you may need to use simulation in order to obtain evidence in relation to responding to dangerous use of ICT equipment and reporting faulty equipment.

Ask your class teacher if you can work with a group of children on a computer programme. Document the kind of assistance you need to give to the children. How does this assistance provide a level of help which

a gives the children the opportunity to develop their self help skills

b maintains their self-confidence and

c enables them to experience a sense of achievement?

As an additional piece of evidence, record what you would do if any of the children began to use equipment dangerously or did not leave it safely or securely after use.

End of unit test

1 What kinds of ICT equipment might be found in primary schools?

2 Name 2 things you should consider when preparing ICT equipment for use.

3 What curriculum area would ICT skills come under in the Foundation Stage?

4 What kinds of ICT programmes might children be using towards the end of Key Stage 2?

5 What should you do if you find any faulty equipment? Should you follow any set procedures?

6 What legislation exists for the use of ICT in schools? What is the main implication of the Data Protection Act 1998?

7 At what age will children start to use the Internet and CD-ROMs in school to support their work?

8 Name 2 ways in which you can support the development of ICT by pupils in schools.

9 How would you find out the kinds of learning packages which are available for the age range with which you are working?

10 What should your school do to prevent viruses when using electronic communication systems such as email?

References

Curriculum Guidance for the Foundation Stage, QCA 2000

National Curriculum Document, QCA 1999

QCA scheme of work for Information Technology, QCA 1998

Websites

BECTA (British Educational Communications and Technology Agency): www.becta.org.uk/technology/software/curriculum/licensing/

National Curriculum Website: www.nc.uk.net

Children Act 1989: www.fnf.org.uk/childact.htm

Data Protection Act: www.hmso.gov.uk/acts/acts1998/19980029.htm

Specialist online schools service: www.learn.co.uk

Appendix

The links between the CACHE Level 2 Certificate for Teaching Assistants (CTA2) and the National Occupational Standards (NVQ)

The CACHE Level 2 Certificate for Teaching Assistants (CTA2) aims to provide an award for candidates who work with pupils individually or in groups under the supervision of a teacher in education and learning support, or who wish to work in this field. The award provides the underpinning knowledge and understanding required for the NVQ Level 2 for Teaching Assistants. Each unit has been mapped against the National Occupational Standards and is shown in the learning of each unit.

The following grid shows this mapping in more detail.

CACHE CTA 2	National Occupational Standards
Unit 1 Supporting the Curriculum	
1 Supporting literacy	2-1, 2-2, 2-3, 2-4, 2-5
2 Supporting mathematics	2-1, 2-2, 2-3, 2-4, 2-5, 3-1, 3-10, 3-11, 3-17
3 Supporting ICT	2-4, 3-1, 3-10, 3-11, 3-17
4 The planning process	2-1, 2-2, 2-3, 2-4, 2-5, 3-1, 3-10, 3-11, 3-17
5 Supporting pupils' learning	2-1, 2-2, 2-3, 2-4, 3-10, 3-11
5 How to scaffold learning on task	2-1, 2-3, 2-4, 2-5, 3-17
Unit 2 Working within the School	
1 The role of the teaching assistant in the school	2-4, 3-11
2 Policies and procedures	2-1, 2-2, 3-11
3 Relationships with pupils	2-2, 3-1, 3-10, 3-11
4 Encouraging positive behaviour	2-2, 2-4, 3-1, 3-10, 3-11

Glossary

Anti-social behaviour – behaviour which harms others or destroys the property or feelings of others.

Appraisal – Process by which staff are required to look at their performance with their line manager and set targets for the coming year.

Autism – a condition which affects an individual's communication skills.

Bilingual/Multilingual children – children who are brought up able to speak more than one language.

Children Act – passed in 1989 to ensure that children's welfare always comes first: applies to storage of information, health and safety, child protection and the rights of the child.

Classroom records – records which are kept on each child by the class teacher on each child's progress.

Classroom layout – the way in which the classroom is organised.

Cognitive Development – the process by which children learn.

Collaborative skills – skills which a team have for working together.

Confidentiality – rules within the school to control the spread of information which may be inappropriate for some people to hear.

Culture – way of life, beliefs and patterns of behaviour which are particular to social groups.

Curriculum Plans – What the teacher plans for children in the long, medium and short term in order to achieve set learning objectives.

Data Protection – means by which information which is held on individuals is protected.

Differentiation – the way in which the class teacher plans to teach children with different abilities.

Disability Discrimination Act – Passed in 1995 to prevent discrimination against disabled people, set to include educational settings from September 2002.

Early Learning goals – expected learning outcomes for the end of the Foundation Stage in the six areas of learning.

Early years settings – settings in which children are educated between the ages of 3 and 5.

Educational psychologist – specialist in children's learning and behaviour.

Emotional development – the development of children's feelings and emotions which enables them to understand and cope with these feelings.

Equal opportunities – ensuring that all individuals have the same opportunities and benefits. Some children may need to have support for this to happen.

Evaluate – to consider whether an activity has achieved its objectives.

Feedback – giving someone information about an activity which has taken place.

Fine motor skills – skills which require more intricate movements, usually with the hands, for example threading beads, controlling a pencil, doing up buttons.

Follow-on tasks – tasks which children can be set following completion of initial learning outcomes, which will reinforce what children have just learned.

Foundation stage – first stage of education, from age 3 to the end of the Reception year.

Gross motor skills – skills which involve the use of larger physical skills, for example running, jumping, throwing.

Individual Education Plan (IEP) – used to plan targets for children who have Special Educational Needs.

Inclusive education – The process by which all children have the right to be educated alongside their peers.

Key Stage 1 – Children's education from the start of Year 1 to the end of Year 2.

Key Stage 2 – Children's education from Year 3 to the end of Year 6.

Language acquisition – the way in which we learn language.

Learning environment – any part of the school where learning takes place.

Learning materials – any materials which are used to support children's learning.

Learning objectives – What the children are expected to know by the end of the lesson.

Literacy hour – Daily lesson in which children work on their reading, writing and speaking and listening skills.

Literacy strategy – government initiative to raise standards of literacy in schools.

National Curriculum – The curriculum for all children aged between 5–16 in England and Wales.

Numeracy hour – Daily lesson for mathematics. It can range from 45 minutes to one hour.

Numeracy strategy – government initiative to raise standards of numeracy in schools.

Observations – watching and making note of children's reactions in learning and play situations.

Occupational therapist – professional who will assess and work with children who have difficulties with fine motor skills.

On task – doing their work.

Open-ended questions – questions which require more than a yes or no answer, for example, 'how did you work that out?'

Parent – a child's birth mother or father or adult who has been given parental responsibility by a court order.

Physiotherapist – professional who will assess and work with children who have difficulties with gross motor skills or body function.

Positive reinforcement – praise given to children to add weight to their achievements.

Professional development – the way in which staff consider and develop their own professional profile.

Pupil records – records which are kept in school regarding each pupil. They may include a number of items such as health details, records of achievement and parents' telephone numbers.

Questioning skills – the way in which children learn to ask questions during their learning.

Resources – items which are available to support learning in school.

Rewards – these can be used to give children additional motivation and can include star charts, marbles in a jar, stickers and choices of activity.

Role – what individuals are required to do as part of their job

School development plan – Document which sets out what the school's priorities will be during the coming year and how they are to be achieved.

School policies – Documents outlining the school's agreed principles in different areas; for example in curriculum areas such as Geography or non-curricular areas, such as behaviour.

Self-esteem – The individual's own perception of his or her worth.

Self-reliance – the individual's ability to do things independently.

SENCo – Special Educational Needs Co-ordinator.

Sensory impairment – an impairment of one or more of the senses.

Settling in procedures – the way in which a school manages children who are entering school or transferring to a different class.

Social development – how a child learns how to live and co-operate with others.

Special Educational Needs (SEN) – Where children are not progressing at the same rate as their peers, they may be said to have SEN.

Speech and language therapist – professional who will assess and work with children with speech and language needs.

Statement of Special Educational Needs – this is given to children who may need additional adult support in school for them to have full access to the curriculum.

Statutory requirements – requirements which have been set down by law.

Stereotyping – generalisation about a group of people which is usually negative and based on a characteristic of one person in that group.

Strategies – how we manage different situations within school

Targets – what children are expected to achieve over a specified period.

Values – an individual's moral principles and beliefs which they feel are important.

Work teams – group of people working together with a common purpose.

Index

A

Abuse, types of 156
access
   to equipment 13
   to computerised information
      222
   to learning environment 13
   to medical care 204
accident forms 190–1
adapting work 33
Additional Literacy Support
   programme (ALS) 116
adjusting to a new setting 193–8
   factors affecting 197
administration of medicines (see
   medicines)
aggression 155
anaphylactic shock 188, 202
anti-bullying policy 165
anti-racism policy 165
appraisal 97–100
   form 99
   good practice 100
assessment, policy 24
assistance
   how to use 74–5
   level of 32
asthma 201
Attention Deficit Hyperactivity
   Disorder (ADHD) 33, 203
attention seeking 155, 156

B

Bandura, Albert 157
behaviour 151–175
   expectations 164
   factors affecting 42, 151–3,
      172
   guidelines for 167
   managing 160, 169
   patterns indicating problems
      42, 154–7
   policy 43, 50, 159, 160, 164–5
   promoting positive 158
   reporting problems 171
   role of adults 163–4
   sanctions for managing 161,
      163, 173
   support plan 34, 174, 175
   theories about 157
behaviour unit 174
behaviour, emotional and social
   development needs 119
Behaviourist theory 65, 157

bilingual children 120–124
   good practice 123
bleeding 188
body language (see non-verbal
   communication)
breathing difficulties (see also
   asthma) 187
bullying 155, 166
burns and scalds 187

C

calculators 133
cardiac arrest 187
caretaker 9
chickenpox 206
child abuse 156
child development 144
   intellectual 150–1
   physical 145–6
   social and emotional
      development 148–9
child protection 43–4, 169
Child protection policy 44, 165
Children Act 1989 26, 43, 169,
   170–1, 179
children's learning
   factors influencing 67–70
   strategies to support 71
   theories of 65
choking 187
circle time 44
classroom equipment (see
   equipment)
classroom layout 7
cognition and learning needs
   118–19
Cognitive Development Theory
   67
commentary 73
common illnesses 206
communication
   good practice 38
   and interaction needs 117
   lines of 87–8
   non-verbal 37
   principles of effective 35–6,
      92
   skills 91
   verbal 36
   within teams 91
computers 212, 214, 218–23
concentration 70–1
confidentiality 24–6, 86, 166,
   204, 219

conflict within teams 95
conjunctivitis 206
courses 100
culture
   awareness of 34
   restrictions due to 190, 207
   valuing a child's 32

D

dangers in learning environment
   16
Data Protection Act 1998 25
Deputy Headteacher, role of 82
development opportunities 100
diabetes 202
diarrhoea 206
differentiation 56, 57
Disability Discrimination Act
   1995 12, 184
disabled children, adapting room
   layout for 13
discipline (see behaviour)
discrimination 12
disruption, causes of 155

E

EAL 120–3
   good practice 123
   problems when supporting 123
   strategies for 120
Early Learning Goals 55, 59, 105
Early Literacy Support programme
   (ELS) 116
educational psychologist 80, 174
electrocution 187
emergencies 187–192
   cultural restrictions 190
   emergency contacts 189
emotional development
   stages of 148–9
   supporting children's 164–5
emotional abuse 156
emotions
   causes of negative 166
   managing 165, 167
   pupils' management of 167
English Policy 105
environment
   adapting for special needs 13
   establishing and maintaining
      safe 177
   planning and equipping 5
epilepsy 187, 202
EpiPen 202, 203, 209

equal opportunities 13, 34
   policy 165
equipment (*see* also resources)
   ICT 211–23, 216
   reporting faults 216
   setting up 213–216
established classes
   joining 195
   transferring 196–7
evaluating 62–64
exchanging information with
  parents 88

F
facilities committee 9
fainting 188
falls 188
farms, visiting 184
feedback (*see* evaluation)
fine motor skills 145
fire
   extinguishers 186
   procedures 185
First Aid 14, 15, 40
   trained First Aiders 204
Foundation Stage 29, 55, 57, 59,
  83, 105, 108
Further Literacy Support
  programme (FLS) 116

G
German measles (rubella) 206
governors 81
gross motor skills 145
group work 45–9
   breakdowns in 49
   dealing with difficulties 49
   good practice 52
   tensions in 49
   types of 45
   working effectively with 45
guided reading 123

H
hazards
   external 183
   identifying potential 181
   internal 179–82
   reporting 177–8
head lice 208
Headteacher, role of 81
Health and Safety
   At Work etc Act 1974 177
   effect on resources 14
   policy 14, 178
   representative 9
   responsibilities 40, 207
Human Rights Act 171
hygiene 199
   supporting hygiene routines 200

I
identifying visitors 184–5
illness 206
impetigo 206
inclusion
   implications of 13
   policy 56, 165
   principles of 11
   promoting 39
independence
   promotion of 31–2
   strategies for 32
Individual Education Plan (IEP)
  21, 34, 174
Individual Support Assistant 39,
  54
information
   keeping information secure
    25, 220
   sharing 23
   within school 87–88
information and communication
  technology (ICT)
   development of skills 220, 221
   equipment 211, 216
   good practice 223
   legislation 219
   policy 218
   safety when using 219, 223
   selecting software 222
injuries 187
inhalers 201–2
intellectual development 150–1
Internet 222

J
job description 39, 85

K
Key Stage managers 82

L
labelling 8
language, stages of development
  35
layout of room 7, 13
learning
   materials 6, 7, 9
   monitoring pupils' response
    75
   objectives 22, 55, 62
learning environment
   adapting 13
   assistant's role in 4
   familiarisation with the 4
   maintaining 8
   resources for 7
   role of others 9–10
legislation (*see also* individual
  Acts)

Children Act 1989 26, 43
Data Protection Act 1998 25
Disability and Discrimination
  Act 1995 12, 184
Health and Safety at Work etc
  Act 1974 177
Human Rights Act 171
SEN and Disability Act 11
letter formation 114
Literacy Strategy 57, 105, 107
Local Education Authorities
  (LEAs) 12, 14, 51

M
managing behaviour (*see*
  behaviour)
maths
   policy 125, 127
   resources 129, 130–2
   vocabulary 132
measles 206
medicines 203
meetings 89–90
meningitis 206
motivation 32, 151
motor skills (*see* fine and gross
  motor skills)
multilingual pupils 120–124

N
National Curriculum 29, 83
National Literacy Strategy (*see*
  Literacy Strategy)
neglect 156
number
   developing understanding of
    127
   good practice 133
Numeracy Strategy 57, 125–7
   key objectives 126

P
parents
   exchange of information 88
   informing of accidents and
    illness 189, 204, 208
Parent-Teachers' Association
  (PTA) 88
pencil grip, correct 113
physical development 146
physical needs 148
physical skills 145
Piaget, Jean
   stages of cognitive
    development 67
planning
   assistant's role in 58–9
   evaluation and assessment 57,
    58
   good practice when 64

long term 58
medium term 58
problems when 61
short term 58, 60
poisoning 187
policies
anti-bullying 44
anti-racism 44
assessment, recording and
reporting 24
behaviour 43, 160, 164
child protection 44
English 105
equal opportunities 43
health and safety 178
ICT 218
inclusion 43, 56, 164
maths 125–127
PSHEC 43, 164, 199
positive reinforcement 65
praise 32, 72,133
preparation of resources 6–8

R
reading
cues for 111
during Literacy Hour 106
with EAL children 121–3
good practice 112
how skills develop 110–11
principles of how children
learn 112
problems when supporting
113
record keeping
roles of other staff 23
role of teaching assistants 24,
62
records
of accidents 23
of health 200–1
keys to good practice 26
from other schools 23
of schemes of work, progress
and assessment 20, 21–2
of special needs, 21, 24
pupil records 19
types of 18
recovery position 188–189
relationships with pupils 30
reporting
accidents 190
hazards 177–8
stock levels 10
suspected abuse 156
resources
availability of 32
examples of 5
for maths activities 129, 132

preparation of 6–8
selecting appropriate 6
ringworm 206
risks, minimising 185
role models 49
roles
of others 80
of teaching assistants 53, 56,
79
of teachers 53, 54
rubella 206
rules (see school rules)

S
safety
cultural restrictions 190
of equipment 181
keys to good practice 17
when using learning materials
181
when managing behaviour
173
policy 178
of self 189
storage 180, 181
sanctions for behaviour 161, 163,
173
school keeper 9
school policies (see policies)
school rules 159
security 16, 184
self-esteem 149, 153
self-fulfilling prophesy theory
157
SEN and Disability Act 2001 11
SENCo 11, 23, 39, 56, 82–3, 98,
140, 174
senior management 82
sensory and physical impairment
119
sexual abuse (see abuse)
shape, space and measures
how pupils develop skills in
134
problems when supporting
137
progression in 134
resources for 136
support strategies for 135–6
shock 188
short term planning (see
planning)
signs and symptoms of illness
205–207
Skinner, Frank 65, 157
social development, stages of 148
Social learning theory 157
speaking and listening
development of skills 108

encouraging 36, 109
helping EAL children 120
good practice 37, 109
in Literacy Hour 106
Special Needs
kinds of 117
records of 24
supporting children with 56,
116–19, 148
Special Educational Needs Co-
ordinator (see SENCo)
speech and language therapist
35
statementing 11, 24, 26, 29, 56
Stepping Stones 59
stereotyping 153
stock, records of 10
subject managers 10, 82
substance abuse 188
supporting pupils
during learning activities 56
good practice when 76
use of praise when 72
supporting teachers 53–64
symptoms of illness (see signs and
symptoms of illness)
swimming pools
safety 183

T
targets 98–9
teams
being part of 91
good practice 94
principles underlying
effectiveness 91, 92–4
problems within 95
relationships within 93
tonsillitis 206
topic plan 22
training needs 87, 100

V
visitors 84, 184–5
voluntary helpers 83
vomiting 206

W
writing
developing skills 113–15
during Literacy Hour 106
with EAL children 121
good practice 114
stages of development 114
strategies for supporting
114–15

Y
year group leader, role 82